THE ROSETTA BONE

BONE

The Key to Communication Between
Canines and Humans

Cheryl S. Smith

HOWELL
BOOK
HOUSE

Howell Book House
Published by Wiley Publishing, Inc., Hoboken, New Jersey
Published simultaneously in Canada

Smith, Cheryl S.
  The Rosetta bone : the key to communication between canines and humans/
by Cheryl S. Smith.
     p. cm.
Includes bibliographical references and index.
  ISBN 0-7645-4421-7 (alk. paper)
  1. Dogs—Training. 2. Dogs—Behavior. 3. Human-animal communication. I. Title.
SF431.S613 2004
636.7'0887—dc22
                                        2003017666

Printed in the United States of America

10 9 8 7 6 5 4 3 2

For Sundance, who taught me how bright and dignified dogs can be;
Spirit, who introduced me to some serious problems with dogs;
Serling, who told me to lighten up and enjoy life;
and Nestle, who speaks a language all his own.

Contents

Preface

This book began as an idea for a humorous little gift book for dog lovers that would take a tongue-in-cheek look at human attempts to communicate with dogs down through the ages and explain how dogs see the world. As I played with the idea and wrote notes for what I wanted to include, however, it became clear that this book wanted to be something more. So the idea mutated into this much longer, more comprehensive, more serious (though, I hope, still fun) book that you hold in your hands.

I've always enjoyed the company of all animals—having at one time or another lived with birds, cats, dogs, snakes, rabbits, turtles, horses, sheep, goats, raccoons and a cow—but I remain particularly attuned to dogs. You can do so many things together, and they like being around us as much as we like being around them. I hope I've learned some things that will help you and your dog live well together.

There are three different kinds of sidebars used throughout the book. The Try It Yourself sidebars are often actual hands-on experiments to try, or sometimes thought experiments to consider. Please stop and actually do whatever is requested, or plan a time to do so if the procedure involves more than yourself and your dog. You can learn a great deal from these little exercises.

You Can Quote Me sidebars are quotes from trainers, behaviorists and veterinarians that are especially pertinent to the subject at hand. Appendix B, Some Quotable People, provides brief profiles of the people who took the time to provide these thought-provoking statements and other input.

The Think About It boxes are sometimes holdovers from the original gift book idea, but more often encouragements to try and help you practice the skill of thinking outside the box. Being able to see a situation from more than one viewpoint is invaluable in dealing with others, whether those others are dogs or humans. These boxes can help you with that goal.

Unless I know the sex of a specific dog mentioned in the book, I refer to dogs as she. This is not because I favor females—I have shared my home with an equal number of males and females—but because I find s/he and her/him to be unacceptably clumsy and because the male construction has had its turn representing everyone.

Although I put the book in an order that makes sense to me, you may prefer to read chapters out of order. This method should present no real problems to readers, other than perhaps having to refer to another chapter for the explanation of some term or technique. However, as you read *The Rosetta Bone*, I hope you will stop often to share what you're reading with your dog. That is, after all, the whole point of the book.

Cheryl S. Smith
June 2003
Port Angeles, Washington

Acknowledgments

It's taken me a long time to learn the information included in this book, and I've had a lot of help along the way. To all the trainers I've ever practiced under, I offer a most sincere thank you. Each one taught me more about what I was doing with dogs. So, to Tom, Rosalie, Emily, Mandy, Mike, Maureen, Terry, Karla and anyone I might have forgotten, I couldn't have gotten here without you.

To APDT (Association of Pet Dog Trainers), Puppyworks and Legacy, who have invited me to conferences galore as a member of the press, you furthered my education—and through my magazine articles and books, the world at large—probably more than you realize. I look forward to many more years of learning.

To everyone who kindly answered my slew of questions via e-mail and phone calls, my most sincere appreciation for your time and sharing of knowledge. A massive thank you to marine mammal trainers/behaviorists Kathy Sdao and Kerrie Haynes-Lovell; veterinarians Karen Overall and Dennis Wilcox; and trainers/lecturers Mandy Book, Morgan Spector, Terry Ryan, Margaret Johnson, Gary Wilkes, Lauren McCall and Debby Potts.

And finally, of course, there are the dogs who have been in my life. They all so perfectly suited my needs at the time each one appeared that it truly boggles the mind, from the first, who needed scarcely any training and was undoubtedly a more complete creature than I at the time, through all the problem children and hard cases, to the softest dog I've ever known, you have all furthered my education, my understanding and indeed my path toward enlightenment. *Cave canem*, indeed—they creep inside you to places you didn't know existed.

CHAPTER I

The Mists of Time

Where did dogs come from?
Where did all those breeds come from?

> It has been 20,000 years since man and dog formed their partnership. That we have altered the dog genetically is well understood; it is hardly known how they changed us. Since dogs could smell and hear better than men, we could concentrate on sight. Since courage is commonplace in dogs, men's adrenal glands could shrink. Dogs, by making us more efficient predators, gave us time to think. In short, dogs civilized us.
>
> Donald McCaig in *Eminent Dogs, Dangerous Men*

The Kato Indians of California have a creation tale like many others . . . up to a point:
The god Nagaicho erected pillars at the four corners of the sky to hold it aloft and expose the earth. With the land exposed, Nagaicho started walking about this new world. He created things as he went, dragging his feet to make the river valleys, bringing forth creatures to fill the spaces. As he walked about, he was accompanied by the dog. Nagaicho didn't create the dog. God had a dog.

THE ANCIENT TIMELINE

Donald McCaig may well be right that dogs civilized us as much as we civilized them, but science indicates the process began much earlier. It's unlikely that we'll ever know precisely when and how the first early humans and the early dog precursors came together. But archaeological evidence demonstrates that the hunting and "home turf" territories of prehistoric man and the wolf overlapped almost constantly. Wolf bones and hominid bones have been found near each other at the cave of Lazaret outside Nice, France, dating back 150,000 years; at the Zhoukoudian site in northern China, going back 300,000 years; and at Kent, England, a site dating back 400,000 years.

This Inuit carving depicts either a wolf or an early sled dog.

Imagine 400,000 years ago, though we were just barely becoming human ourselves, we were already sharing our space with canines. Lazaret shows some sort of intentional thought toward the wolf, at least—each individual shelter within the cave had a wolf skull carefully placed at its entrance.

Perhaps it shouldn't be surprising that our association with dogs is so ancient. Behaviors that seem to echo our own always interest us. We've always tended to live in "packs" (our family units or tribes), and we value loyalty to the pack. Using these values, wolves would naturally seem attractive fellow travelers, living together cooperatively, caring for their young.

We weren't necessarily the driving force behind the coming together of humans and wolves, soon to be dogs. Wolves, with their hierarchy of subordinance (it's safer to think of their relationships as subordinance rather than dominance, as you'll see when we talk about much later human-dog interactions), needed to develop noninjurious ways to communicate willingness to follow rather than lead. A pack wouldn't survive if members were constantly being injured in ranking quarrels, after all. So they became experts at reading situations and defusing threats. Being such highly effective social predators, they could extend their own system to that of others in their environment, notably, humans.

Though no one knows exactly how actual domestication came about, a process of "mutual domestication," with man and wolf adopting each other, seems at least as likely as any other explanation. It's even

Cave art representation of a hunter working with his dogs.

possible that the wolf chose us, and there wasn't much we could do to "keep the wolf from the door" once he decided to settle in.

The best evidence thus far places the time the human and wolf joined forces at the point when humans shifted from a hunter/gatherer lifestyle to a partly settled agricultural lifestyle. That would place us somewhere around the 20,000 years ago Donald McCaig was talking about at the beginning of this chapter.

The earliest remains identified fairly definitively as dog rather than wolf come from Oberkassel, Germany, dating back 14,000 years. Recognizable changes in the skull—shorter jaw, defined stop (the drop from forehead to muzzle, in front of the eyes)—and generally smaller size tell archaeologists they're not dealing with wolf remains here. Because the wolf didn't become a dog overnight, and odds are we haven't happened upon the oldest evidence, 20,000 years ago sounds like a reasonable guess, and it's a nice round number.

Other sites from approximately the same period have been found scattered around Iraq and Israel. One of the Israeli sites at Ein Mallaha included a tomb that held the skeleton of an aged woman,

What might the Rosetta Bone look like? Haven't you longed for a better way to talk to your dog, a known-to-unknown language translation? Unfortunately, there is no Rosetta Stone for Doglish, but we'll come as close as we can.

placed with her hand over the chest of the skeleton of a puppy. The juxtaposition of human and canine fairly shouts of an affectionate relationship.

At this time, hunting strategy was changing from an up-close encounter between the beast and humans wielding heavy stone axes to a longer-distance affair with bows and arrows tipped with tiny stone blades. The drawback to this new technique was that the beasts often were only wounded and could escape. Having dogs, even barely domesticated ones, that could track down the wounded prey would have made this method much more efficient. Without the help of dogs, humans might have discarded the bow and arrow as inefficient.

By the time humans were tilling the land, perhaps about 9,000 years ago, dogs were everywhere. Remains have been found scattered around the world. The Koster site in Illinois includes evidence of an 8,500-year-old pet cemetery, and even as early as this, different types of dogs were starting to emerge in different regions.

THEORIES OF DOMESTICATION

Various theories exist about how domestication occurred. Some hypothesize that early humans took wolf pups from their dens. Some might have been immediately skinned and eaten, but others could have been held for a later feast. Perhaps a harried mother noticed that the pups kept her own offspring occupied while she tried to prepare skins.

Another theory, supported by the activities of current-day South American aboriginal peoples, is that humans are born pet keepers, and the first wolves brought into camps were meant to be nothing more than pets. Today's South American tribes bring home the young of animals they kill and keep them as pets. Once the animals have names, they do not end up as dinner or ritual sacrifices.

A third theory of canine domestication relies more on a sort of co-domestication. Both wolves and primitive humans used a wide-ranging group hunting style, and probably preyed on many of the same species. Their paths undoubtedly crossed often. Wolves may have realized that humans sometimes wounded prey but did not kill it, and the wolves had the advantage in tracking and finishing off the wounded animal. A pack could have adopted the strategy of follow-ing human hunting parties. (It could just as easily have been exactly the opposite, the humans following wolves, letting them make the kill and then driving them off and claiming the prize.)

This tomb painting at Beni-Hassan dates from approximately 2100 B.C.

The currently popular hypothesis comes from biologist Ray Coppinger, who sees the first contact being made by wolves scavenging human dump sites. The lowest-ranking wolves, the omegas, often couldn't get enough to eat with the pack. Being subservient and used to taking orders from everyone, and needing to eat, these wolves would tend to have more tolerance of human proximity. Their scavenging activities helped decrease odors from refuse, attracting fewer rats and larger unwanted visitors and even averting some pestilence. Human habitations with a resident wolf or two may have benefited from an early warning system as wolves alerted them to approaching danger. Barking came later, as wolves turned into dogs, but even wolves raise a fuss when their territory is threatened. So the early humans let them stay. Just as with captive wolves today, one or two pups out of each litter probably showed a lower tendency to flee from humans, moving toward the symbiotic relationship we share today.

ANCESTORS OF THE DOG

As researchers have tried to determine the progenitor of the domestic dog, the most-often mentioned candidates have been the wolf and the jackal, but scientists propose others as well. Based on the number of chromosomes in DNA specimens, there are five logical choices:

1. Grey wolf, *Canis lupus*, ranging across most of the northern hemisphere
2. Golden jackal, *Canis aureus*, once throughout the Old World
3. Coyote, *Canis iatrans*, throughout North America
4. African wild dog, *Lycaon pictus*, in sub-Saharan Africa
5. Dhole, *Cuon alpinus*, formerly across Asia

All of these animals have 78 chromosomes, the same as the dog. However, the African wild dog and the Dhole cannot interbreed with the dog and produce fertile offspring, so that deletes them from the list. Examining patterns of behavior provides another clue. Veterinary behaviorist Bonnie Beaver notes that wolves and dogs share 71 of 90 charted behavioral patterns, more than any other two canid species.

Painted representation of Anubis, Queen Hatshepsut's Temple, Egypt. These Egyptian representations may have been part of the reason the jackal was thought to be a progenitor of the dog.

DNA research by Dr. Robert Wayne of UCLA indicates four major groups of dog DNA, all related to wolf populations and indicating four domestication "events" in history. One of these DNA groups is much larger than the others, covering three-quarters of our dog breeds today. It contains all of the more "primitive" dog types, such as the New Guinea singing dog, Indian pariah dogs and Greyhounds. A second group, though smaller, covers most of the remaining breeds and seems to be relatively younger, indicating a more recent domestication event. The other two groups are tiny and negligible.

There are 32 subspecies of *Canis lupus*, so limiting the dog to one ancestor—rather than the frequently postulated "some from wolves, some from jackals, some from foxes" theory—does not preclude the immense variety of sizes and shapes of dogs.

Part of the domestication question must consider exactly what differentiates a wild wolf from a domestic dog. Generally, domesticated mammals tend to become smaller in size with changes in the color and markings of their coats. In the case of dogs, their jaws became shortened, making their teeth both smaller and more crowded, and they developed a pronounced "stop," the drop from the front of the forehead to the muzzle. They also developed characteristics that don't show up in the archaeological record, such as hanging ears and a much greater propensity to bark. In many dogs, the skull became more domed and the eyes grew larger. Many of these physical changes, as well as behavioral characteristics retained from juvenile wolves—increased seeking of social contacts, submissive food begging, relative lack of fear, active periods throughout the day—made the dog appear more "puppylike" and hence more appealing to human eyes.

In fact, veterinarian David Paxton claims that once early humans had the wolves' keener senses to rely on, humans could give up some of their own abilities. He theorizes that with a decreased need for an acute sense of smell, the human face became flatter and developed a vastly more mobile mouth and lips. By tracing this path, he credits the domestication of the dog with the development of human speech.

EGYPT AND OTHER ANCIENT CIVILIZATIONS

The Egyptians seemed to have a real knack for taming animals and kept a variety of pets. They often receive credit for the domestication of the cat, but dogs figured into their lives as well. Many canines prance across tomb paintings. They have been variously identified as Greyhounds, Salukis, Pharaoh Hounds, Canaan Dogs and Ibizan Hounds. All of these current breeds may indeed have descended from these Egyptian dogs, often pictured hunting with their masters.

Less frequently portrayed were small short-legged dogs. When they do appear, the setting is usually domestic, so they may have been watchdogs, destroyers of vermin in the home or simply pets.

Assyrian artwork of this period depicts large heavy dogs that resemble Mastiffs. They are shown fighting in battles, serving as guard dogs and hunting. One of the many Egyptian

A reproduction of a funerary jar with the head of Anubis, into which the mummified person's internal organs were placed.

deities, Anubis, bears the head of a jackal or dog. Anubis guarded the way to the underworld of the dead. Taking the connection between dogs and death a step further, some ancient civilizations believed that a human soul could not reach the other side unless it first passed through a dog, so bodies were left out for dogs to devour. As gruesome as that sounds, it may have helped prevent the spread of disease. The Greeks believed dogs could play a role in warding off death, and they kept dogs as therapists in their healing temples, as givers of therapeutic dreams and providers of licks deemed to be healing.

Carved representations of Anubis (later partially obliterated) appear at the Temple of Horus, Egypt.

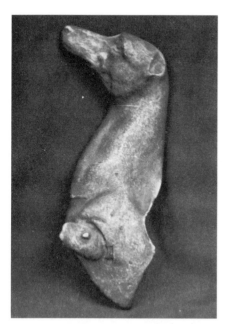

This reproduction of the armpiece of a Greek couch clearly represents a Greyhound.

The Romans were also wild about dogs, and seem to have realized that by choosing dogs to mate based on appearance or behavior they could develop specific abilities. They had guard dogs and dogs who fought in battle, as well as dogs who hunted by sight and others who hunted by scent. They also had a variety of house dogs, including lap dogs of a distinctly Maltese type. In fact, some say that the *cave canem* ("Beware of the dog") signs found outside dwellings in Pompeii and Rome were not to warn visitors that the house dogs might bite, but to caution them not to step on the little Italian Greyhounds inside.

The Chinese emperors also kept pets. Their puppies had human wet nurses and adult dogs had their own servants. The Pekingese exists as a breed from at least A.D. 700, developed to resemble the spirit lion (who could avert evil and bring good fortune) of the Buddhist religion (its appearance has changed markedly in modern times). Pekingese and other small breeds were known as *ch'in*, or sleeve dogs. They were carried about in the voluminous sleeves of their

This Chinese incense burner features a lion dog.

owners, both for a little added warmth and to lure fleas away from their masters. Individual Pekingese were often entombed with their emperors, and ancient imperial dog cemeteries are scattered about Beijing.

STEPPING FORWARD—DARK AGES, MIDDLE AGES AND BEYOND

Dogs (and other pets) experienced bewildering changes in attitudes during the Middle Ages. First, the nobility—who controlled nearly all the land suitable for hunting—viewed the hunt as an important symbol of status. Separate breeds were developed to hunt nearly every individual animal quarry. There were Foxhounds, Deerhounds, Otterhounds and Wolfhounds, as well as the coursing Greyhounds and trailing Bloodhounds. Commoners were banned from owning either Greyhounds or Bloodhounds, and causing the death of a Greyhound was akin to murder. Greyhounds appeared often as heraldic symbols, and were featured in Chaucer's 14th-century *Canterbury Tales*. Poachers developed the half-Greyhound Lurcher, still popular in England today, to hunt silently and swiftly where they were not welcome.

During this era, humans began to recognize the dog's many additional functions. A Chinese scroll from the 13th century called "Spring on the Yellow River" shows a small dog leading a blind man. Various other attempts to use the dog as a guide for the blind appear in Western literature throughout the 14th century.

In the midst of all this development, the medieval church stirred itself to action. Its stated reason for being against the keeping of pets was that excess food should be given to the poor, not to animals. The real reasons for disapproval ran much deeper. The Christian view of the world was God supreme, man below him, then everything else existing to serve man. When the Bible mentions the dog it is not as a companion but as a dirty, unworthy beast. Determined to separate man from "unreasoning beast," the Church railed against pet keeping. Then, in a darker turn, close association with animals became branded as a sign of pagan worship. The Inquisition often needed no more proof than a pet dog or cat to declare someone a heretic.

This Chinese snuff bottle features clearly recognizable spaniels.

In Genesis, God declares that man has "dominion" over every living thing. In the 13th century, the Christian theologian Thomas Aquinas translated the works of ancient Greeks such as Aristotle and Plato. Their classical ideas meshed well with Christian theology, putting Greek men at the apex of the "ladder of life," with Greek women and other free peoples on the next rung, slaves and "barbarians" the next rung down, animals scattered down the next several rungs and plants below them. All the lower rungs were naturally meant to serve all the rungs above them.

Note the creatures with curled tails, almost certainly dogs, in these petroglyphs on the island of Lanai, Hawaii.

Pope Gregory IX called for a purge of pet animals in 1233. Cats, dogs, birds and others were tortured, put on trial, found guilty, excommunicated and publicly executed. The infamous witch trials of the 16th and 17th centuries spread across Europe and later sprang up again in North America. Many of the accused were elderly, socially isolated women of limited means, who probably kept pets for companionship. In the trials, however, such pets became "animal familiars," symbols of Satan. The names by which the "devil" is referred to in transcripts of witch trials seem decidedly unhorrific: Rutterkin, Bunne, Pretty. They seem more like, well, pet names. Further reading reveals that they are just that, despite attempts by the Inquisitors to disguise the fact. The devil is found in "the likeness of a little white Dog" and in the soft fur of the "kittin."

But the human urge to keep pets seemed overpowering. Even nuns were guilty of it, and manuscript illustrators worked cheerful dogs and cats into their designs again and again. St. Francis, who reportedly had the ability to tame wild animals with a mere glance and now serves as the patron saint of ecologists, preached during this time as well. Try as they might, the Church could not stamp out the keeping of pets. Partly this may be due to human nature, and partly the persistence of dogs themselves. Jonica Newby notes in *The Animal Attraction* that dogs are present today even in societies where they are shunned or eaten. The Church was waging a losing battle.

By the time of the Renaissance, the Church's efforts had waned, and nobility was again reveling in the keeping of pets. Henry III of France kept as many as 2,000 lap dogs, who lived (literally) in the lap of luxury. Louis XIV spent 200,000 gold francs for construction of the royal kennels at Versailles, where he kenneled hunting hounds, truffle terriers and Toy Poodles. The Medicis raised Papillons and Bolognese. Shakespeare gave King Lear a loyal dog named Sweetheart. And Tsunayoshi, known as the Dog Shogun, nearly plunged Japan into bankruptcy to feed his 100,000 dogs.

Life wasn't necessarily all joy for companion animals, however. In line with Church teachings, René Descartes declared that animals were unemotional objects, things, machines. Because they did not have the ability to reason, he said, they could not suffer. The piercing screams of animals undergoing the horrors of vivisection were deemed to be no more than the mechanical sounds of a clockwork device running down. The prevalent theology of the time had indoctrinated many to feel no obligation or empathy toward any of the other beings upon the earth.

There was also the issue of using dogs as labor. While hunting across the fields and forests of earls and dukes may have been fun for packs of hounds, other canines toiled at less enjoyable tasks. Small dogs were placed in devices resembling a larger version of today's hamster wheels and were forced to trot for hours at a time, propelling a bar to turn a roast over a fire. Named for their job, the dogs were referred to as turnspits. Other, larger dogs hauled carts through the streets of the fast-rising cities, delivering milk, bread and other merchandise. When not engaged in these tasks, dogs were expected to guard the home, destroy vermin, protect the flocks or serve as living foot warmers during long and chilly church services (probably one of their most enjoyable tasks, since they weren't required to do anything other than lie still).

Dogs also took part in the expansion of the empire that rocketed along during the Renaissance. Mastiff war dogs accompanied the conquistadors to the Americas, where they were fearsome weapons indeed. The Native Americans had their own dogs as well. A few tribes used them in battle, but more often they were pack animals, ceremonial sacrifices or even a food supply. In the Pacific Northwest, Native Americans even kept purpose-bred dogs referred to as "wool dogs." These small white fluffy dogs were sheared like sheep for fiber. Some tribes went so far as to keep these dogs on islands so that they couldn't interbreed with the more coyote-like camp dogs.

Back in Europe, feudalism was coming to an end and commoners were freer to move about and live their own lives. Many migrated from the country to the city, where some managed to make a decent living, and the middle class began to develop. Increasing populations required more cleared agricultural lands and more dogs to keep control of the vermin that came with the new fields. In England, Oliver Cromwell and the anti-pet Puritans gave way to Charles II, who raised King Charles Toy Spaniels. The British imported the Pug from China. One of Sir Isaac Newton's lesser-known achievements was the invention of the cat door, which was soon adapted to serve dogs. Dogs were favorite subjects for artists and appear in many portraits and landscapes of the time. Dogs were everywhere.

ALMOST MODERN

With the rise of the Victorian era, the proliferation of breeds began in earnest. The desire to keep pets as a link with the natural world coincided with Darwin's revolutionary *Origin of Species*. With this greater knowledge of the laws of inheritance, dog breeding became much more formalized. Though the upper crust still considered it inappropriate for the "lower classes" to neglect their social duties by frittering away time on pets, their opinion no longer carried much weight. Even the roughest workman was likely to have a dog of some sort. The Industrial Revolution meant more wealth and free time for many. The idea of paying to use a particular dog as a stud first sprang into being.

Coursing meets, long popular among the nobility, became both more formal and more accessible. The first dog show was held at London's Crystal Palace in 1873, the same year the (English) Kennel Club was founded. The American Kennel Club followed soon after. In order to judge dogs, official breed standards were written. They paid much attention to details of coat, coloring, ears and such and gave horrifyingly little heed to temperament. And so it has continued, right up to the present day. Now breeders realize a greater need to consider health, both physical and mental, along with looks, but it will take some time to correct mistakes already made, and dedication to avoid making new ones.

As more dog competitions arose, more dog owners became involved in training their canines. Techniques were often harsh, though in the 1920s and '30s, food training flourished briefly. Military use of the dog quickly swung training back to methods of force— trainers relied on choke collars, pinch collars and the need to "dominate" the dog. The lines of communication were one-way only, master to dog. Though some compassionate handlers may have been more even-handed, the training books and manuals warn against "disobedience," "bids for dominance" and "unwillingness to work." It was very much a reflection of the military's philosophy that you first have to break down a recruit before you can train him.

Finally, near the end of the 20th century, the pendulum swung back. Puppy classes were introduced. Puppies were too soft and impressionable to be jerked around by collars, so trainers had to use other methods. Food training was reborn, and clicker training made the leap from marine mammal trainers to dog trainers. People became interested in how the dog might feel about training. The lines of communication began to open.

CHAPTER 2

Wagging Tongues, Wagging Tails

Why should you want to communicate?
Why should your dog want to listen?

> 'Tis sweet to hear the watch dogs' honest bark
> Bay deep-mouthed welcome as we draw near home;
> 'Tis sweet to know there is an eye will mark
> Our coming and look brighter when we come.
>
> Lord Byron, *Don Juan*, Canto I
> (Byron is also famous for his epitaph "To Boatswain," his
> Newfoundland—you can read it at the beginning of
> Chapter 3, Conversation With a Canine.)

You don't have to attend a lecture by some high-powered motivational guru to understand what a failure to communicate can mean. Consider this situation: You're trying to learn a new software program. Your continued employment depends on it, and you don't have much time. Your manager, Dirk, stands behind you, directing your efforts. The first time you make a mistake, Dirk yells "No!" and slaps you on the ear. This doesn't exactly lower your anxiety, and you make more mistakes. The yelling gets progressively louder and the slaps get harder. If you're a naturally timid sort, pretty soon you're afraid to touch another key and earn yourself another smack on the head. If you're more assertive, you just might turn around and punch Dirk in response to the next slap. In either case, how likely are you to learn the software and keep your job?

So what does this have to do with communicating with your dog? Putting a choke collar on your dog and jerking him around for not sitting when told—even though the dog doesn't have a clue what "sit"

17

Think About It

From ancient China comes this legend of two brothers. The first complained about his dog.

"I left the house yesterday morning dressed all in white. When I returned home I was clothed in black. My dog barked at me because he is so stupid that he could not recognize me wearing black."

The man's brother, a renowned philosopher, rarely answered quickly, and considered before he spoke. Then he asked this question.

"If your dog were the one leaving in the morning, a solid white dog, and he came back that night solid black, would you recognize him?"

How would you answer the philosopher's question? Would you fare any better than the dog?

means—amounts to the same situation as you and manager Dirk. You and the dog are both being punished simply for your lack of knowledge.

Far too often, we humans expect our dogs to understand what we say to them, without any effort on our part. We're all guilty of being manager Dirk. And worse, some of us accuse our dogs of being stupid when they don't understand.

Dogs are easy to talk to.

You Can Quote Me

For real communication to occur between yourself and your dog, you need to know exactly what you are saying and how it will be received by your dog. In a world where animals and humans coexist, it's important to realize that ignorance of their language is no excuse.

Gary Wilkes, columnist and founder of Click & Treat

WHY SHOULD YOU WANT TO COMMUNICATE?

One may as well ask, "Why did you get a dog?" There are people in this world who keep dogs chained in the yard without any more interaction than bringing them food and water, but this isn't a lifestyle I can condone or even comprehend. Dogs make such remarkable companions for humans that wasting their talents seems nearly criminal. Though I would be the first to admit that I'm probably more dog-obsessed than most (I not only love their company, I make my living writing about them, after all), everyone should aspire to a good, workable level of interspecies communication.

As veterinarian, animal behaviorist and dog trainer Ian Dunbar points out, dogs are animals with a variety of natural behaviors. They chew, they dig, they bark, they pee and poop. Owners must explain where they want their dogs to pee and poop, what they are allowed to chew, when and for how long they can bark. In short, owners have the responsibility for explaining the house rules to the dog *and* providing an acceptable outlet for natural doggy activities. Note that there are two parts to this process. Asking a terrier, bred down through the ages to tunnel into the ground in pursuit of rodents, not to dig goes so much against the dog's ingrained instincts that other problems may arise out of stress induced in the dog. Giving the dog a place where digging is encouraged makes for a hole-free yard and a contented dog.

Perhaps, historically, people could blithely ignore communication with the dog because any consequences nearly always fell on the dog. A dog left to run loose would be hit by a car, a dog who bit a kid was killed and an unwanted litter would be dumped in the woods or thrown in a pond. But now, with everyone seemingly intent on suing everyone else, consequences have come along for the humans involved, too. Now if a dog bites a kid, the dog may still pay with his or her life, but the owner may also be parting with cold hard cash. Loose-running dogs can be picked up by animal control and the owners fined.

Should monetary penalties figure into making people communicate with their dogs? No! But if it results in a better bond between more people and their dogs, then bring on the fines! After all, if the problems that send dogs to shelters, even to their deaths, are nothing more than natural behaviors occurring in inappropriate places or ways, the root of the problem is miscommunication or lack of communication. You simply can't have conflict resolution without communication.

Communicating with other people can be a difficult undertaking—why should some expect it to be effortless with their dogs? Yet most of us talk to our dogs all the time. It's so much a part of our makeup that when Professor Aaron Katcher of the University of Pennsylvania, an expert on the social effects of pets on his human patients, was setting up a research project to investigate the physiological effects of pets on humans, his graduate student pointed out that his design wouldn't work. The student noted that subjects were supposed to sit quietly with their pets—but no one sits with a pet without talking to the pet! The research design was modified.

Though we may talk to our pets a lot, we aren't necessarily communicating. We need to take a look at both how our dogs understand

 You Can Quote Me

Do I think most dog owners make sufficient allowance for their dog's wants and needs? No, and I think the number of dogs in our nation's shelters and killed for normal canine behaviors—digging, chewing, barking, etc.—bears that out. I don't think most people are mean. I think it's mostly miscommunication between two species. I think if we had more trained dogs in our country, we'd have a lot less dead ones.

Margaret Johnson, author and trainer

Try It Yourself

Think it's hard to communicate with another species? Try this experiment. Wait until your dog is dozing somewhere in the house other than the kitchen. Go to the kitchen and do whatever signals food to your dog—open the "meats" drawer in the refrigerator, whirr the can opener or pull open a bag of chips. Odds are good you will have four-footed company in the kitchen in the matter of a few microseconds. That's effective communication, and probably not anything you ever set out to teach the dog.

us and what the dog is communicating back. When you open up the channels of communication, you will find that you possess more influence over your dog's behavior without having to resort to punishment of any sort. Good news, indeed, to all but a few inveterate drill-sergeant types. Certainly, good news to our dogs.

Do not be swayed by arguments of the extremists of the animal rights movement that it is cruel to "impose our will" on our canine friends. Is it cruel to toilet train your children, to advise them to say "please" and "thank you" and to equip them to play well with others? Dogs live in our human community. Many are so far removed from their wild forebears that they could not fend for themselves. They provide us with beauty, unswerving loyalty and a needed connection with nature. Our part of the bargain is to provide food, care, mental stimulation and the social graces needed to live well in our world.

In talking with other dog owners and trainers, I've learned that a lot of us seem to follow similar paths to communication enlightenment. So my own tale may prove illuminating.

I had two large black dogs when I first started a serious training program. Though the male, Serling, was friendliness personified and the female, Spirit, was truly psychotic (victim of a puppy mill breeding and a pet store upbringing), their training was the same—choke collars and "pops" with the leash. I was new enough and susceptible enough to "authority" that it didn't occur to me to question this. So we went on for several months, until Serling earned his CD

(Companion Dog, the first level of obedience title) and advanced to the Open class.

Both my dogs were natural-born retrievers and would fetch tennis balls or sticks by the hour. So the instruction I was given—to administer an ear pinch as I told Serling to retrieve—was puzzling, to say the least. He strained against my hold on his collar to go fetch. Why should I punish him before even giving him a chance to do it right? Because he would never be reliable otherwise, I was told. After hearing that unsatisfying answer, I was even more intent on getting to the bottom of why I should punish Serling in this manner. This theory of training applied to everything I had been doing since my dogs and I had starting training together. This was my dog training epiphany.

I never did ear-pinch Serling. He achieved his CDX (Companion Dog Excellent, the second-level obedience title) with one High in Trial award and no problem on the retrieve. Our success gave me faith that I was onto something, and I looked for a different way to train. Thanks to innovators such as Ian Dunbar, Karen Pryor, Terry Ryan and others, there was another way for all of us to go—a way of relying on honest communication in both directions.

As trainers began using this new method, we found that results came faster and responses were more reliable. All that jerking on the leash wasn't necessary. Certainly, no ear-pinching was required. The big surprise (though perhaps it shouldn't have been) was the attitude of the dogs. They *wanted* to be trained! They asked for—in some cases nearly demanded—training sessions. Initial learning of

---

 You Can Quote Me

Dogs pay attention to *our* behavior. They're looking at us and looking at us because this is how they communicate. The dog is integrating our nonverbal communication nonstop all day long. They meet our needs, but we're less concerned with meeting theirs. One of the things that we have to begin to get people to think about is their dog's needs independent of them, their dogs as individuals who are not small fuzzy humans.

Karen Overall, veterinarian, columnist and animal behaviorist

You Can Quote Me

Our interactions with them [dogs] must seem unbelievably coarse at times to these sophisticates of nonverbal communication. Our responsibility as handlers is to attempt to be as skilled in our observations and nonverbal communications with our dogs as they are in their interactions with us.

Suzanne Clothier, author of *Body Posture and Emotions*

new commands or exercises progressed at light speed compared to the old "jerk and praise." Well, wouldn't you work harder for someone who told you how well you were doing and gave you a bonus than for old ear-slapping manager Dirk?

For real dog people, part of the point of having a dog lies in trying to understand a different species day by day. The undertaking opens up new ways of looking at the world. In fact, those involved with their dogs often report a growing talent for "thinking outside the box" and increasing success in their employment. Dogs encourage problem-solving prowess that extends beyond their own concerns.

All reports indicate that dogs are better at interspecies communication than we are. Canine society is based on the hierarchy of subordinance, mentioned in Chapter 1, The Mists of Time. To maintain order and amiable relations without bloodshed, canines—both wolves and dogs—have developed exquisitely subtle social cues. The flick of an ear, blink of an eye or wave of a tail can threaten violence, signal submission and resolve an incipient conflict with cues so fine they could be missed completely if canines weren't so attentive to them.

So what do you see when you really try to understand your dog? Some scientists state that there are no rigorous, controlled studies to prove that dogs have emotions. But some will admit privately, and a few brave souls will assert publicly, that the anecdotal evidence is overwhelming. Dog aficionados don't need controlled studies. They have no doubt that their dogs can be happy or sad, self-assured or fearful. Some have a sense of humor. Of course, there's also that most-touted asset of the canine species, loyalty.

This denial of emotions in other animals is a hangover from the days of Descartes, a human defensive mechanism to justify the way we have treated animals (and in some cases, still are treating them). In fact, there was a time when even some subgroups of humans were branded as subhuman, incapable of feeling the "higher" emotions. Don't buy into this Old-World smoke screen. Thousands of years of dog evolution have taken the wolf's excellence at socially effective behavior and fine-tuned those social behaviors to work on humans.

I know, without a shadow of a doubt, that dogs have emotions. If we can't even be sure what another person is feeling, what makes us think we can be so sure that dogs feel nothing? The problem comes from using the same words for dog feelings that we use to describe human emotions. We are trapped in our verbal world, trying to fit precise definitions to imprecise concepts. Some might sneer if we say, "My dog loves me," but we might get away with saying, "My dog enjoys my company and is happier when I'm around." I can withstand

When dogs listen, they really listen.

No, this isn't a two-headed dog. But note how the dog in front is listening to whatever the dog in back finds so interesting (see where his ears are pointing?), but is looking at something else. Dogs' mobile ears give them this advantage.

some derision from the non-doggy crowd—I make no bones about it, my dog loves me. Exactly how that word applies to my dog's feelings toward me I can't explain, but it's the best word I have.

Because you are reading this book, the odds are good that you already believe your dog has emotions and don't need any convincing. With that as a given, improving your communication with your dog can deepen the bond and strengthen those emotions. After a year or two of working together, you might find yourselves like an old married couple, knowing what the other is going to do before anyone makes a move.

So, why should you want to communicate? To make living together more rewarding, to accomplish training more quickly and easily, to have a more willing canine partner and to share a deeper bond. Good enough reasons for you?

WHY SHOULD YOUR DOG WANT TO LISTEN?

If you have any sort of relationship with your dog, the dog understands that most consequences, both good and bad, come from you.

Try It Youself

How is your communication with your dog? Try these exercises.

1. With your dog in the room, but without saying anything, get down on the floor. Sit there quietly. Does your dog:

   a. run over to you and give you an enthusiastic face-washing?

   b. look at you for a second, then roll over and go back to sleep?

   c. run out of the room and peek at you from around the corner?

   Contrary to what you might think, none of these answers is automatically bad. Context counts. So, if you ordinarily sit on the floor to clip your dog's nails (as I do), then "c" might be a logical response on your dog's part. However, the dog should come over to you willingly if you call. If you're in the habit of sitting on the floor to watch television, usually with no consequences for the dog, then "b" is a perfectly acceptable response. Result "a" could mean that you have a great relationship with your dog (and find face licking acceptable—some do and some don't) or you're a doormat and your dog walks all over you.

Dogs, though they are lovable and loyal and all those wonderful things, excel at looking out for number one. Given any chance at all, dogs will make it their business to listen and learn.

Although we love our dogs, we impose a plethora of rules on them—rules that make no particular sense to a canine way of life. Still, dogs are willing to go along with pretty much whatever rules we want to make, if only we'll explain ourselves clearly.

In explaining ourselves clearly, we have to realize that we're dealing with an animal who doesn't understand our language. So your language has to be basic and easily understood. With dogs, that translates best as simple positives and negatives—rewards and reprimands.

Rewards and reprimands sound simple enough. But there's a little more to it. For effective communication, both rewards and reprimands

2. After some time has passed, try this experiment again, but this time put a terrible scowl on your face as you sit on the floor. Does your dog's response change?

   Dogs study us intently. We are, after all, in charge of many aspects of their lives, and they are astonishingly good at picking up cues about what is in the offing for them. If you put on a convincing scowl, the face-licking dog probably did not approach you this time; the unconcerned dog may have gotten up and left the room or remained in place but stared at you; and the dog who left the room may not have hung around to peek around the corner.

3. Try it again, but this time with a big smile and loose and happy body language, sort of as if you're bopping to a happy song. Odds are good that no matter what the initial response from the dog was, this time the dog will come over to you.

Think about this when you're trying to communicate with the dog. A lot more than *what* you're saying matters.

must be real, relevant and reliable. "Real" goes hand in hand with relevant and reliable in various ways, so we'll discuss this in two parts.

Making It Relevant

You can't explain to the dog that if he doesn't stop chewing the furniture, he's headed to the animal shelter. This is a creature who doesn't understand single words (until you've educated him or her), let alone entire sentences. Fuzzy ideas of future consequences are useless.

Real, concrete consequences are relevant. For the dog, these could include:

- Food (and water)
- Freedom (off-leash opportunities)

- Attention (praise or pats)
- Play
- Avoidance of aversives (reprimands)
- Opportunity to socialize
- Control of possessions

All of these can be manipulated by dog owners to serve as rewards. Most owners find food the most consistently useful choice (though specific situations might call for other options, and some dogs are not highly food-motivated). Food works so well because it's one of the basic necessities of life. It's *really* relevant. All living creatures have a strong drive to procure food. Of course, dogs lucky enough to be members of families have their food provided by their humans. That doesn't mean you have to just fill up the bowl and present it to the dog every day. You can make the dog earn every last piece of kibble if you want.

Don't fall into the trap of only using food as a reward. You will be a much more exciting and inspirational communicator/trainer if you are somewhat unpredictable. In fact, the more you interact with your dog, the more options you will discover for rewards. The more options you have, the better the chance that you will have the perfect one to use in any given situation.

My own dog, Nestle, gets rewarded in agility training with the chance to play with another dog after a particularly tricky exercise. It's an extra-special treat in addition to my usual food rewards and praise.

 You Can Quote Me

Each time you ask your dog to do something, imagine him looking back at you and asking you "Why should I?" It is a very good question indeed. How well you can answer that reasonable question by making clear to the dog what the relevance of this activity is will determine how successful you are in your training.

Suzanne Clothier, author of *Finding a Balance*

Think About It

You're working your dog and the dog has just given you a great performance. You want to give a great reward. But you are out of food, don't have any toys at hand and are victim of a sudden attack of laryngitis. What can you do?

If you said you'd just pet your dog, that's sort of a ho-hum reward. Here are some more exciting possibilities:

- In a safe, fenced area, let the dog off leash and play a rousing game of chase. Lots of dogs love to play chase and keep-away and often try to initiate this fun game with no response from their humans.
- If your dog is a retriever, throw your empty bait bag if you wear one, your wallet, whatever you have handy (though not your keys unless they have a cloth or leather keychain—dogs don't generally like to pick up metal).
- Offer your dog a play bow. You don't have to actually get down on your knees and put your forearms on the ground. Most dogs better recognize your meaning if you lower your head and shoulders, smile and lunge toward them.
- Jump up and down, clap your hands and run around in little circles.
- One that requires pretraining, but is always available (except for really large dogs)—teach your dog to jump into your arms. I've seen conformation handlers use this for dogs as large as Siberian Huskies.

Use your imagination! Think like a dog!

When considering rewards, don't forget about rewards that are inherent to the dog's action. For example, for a dog who's nervous when left alone, chewing on something reduces stress. The chewing itself is a rewarding activity because it makes the dog feel better. The consequences when the owner comes home are totally disconnected from the act of chewing (and a great mystery to the dog). A dog that goes into trash cans is frequently rewarded by finding something tasty (at least to the dog's way of thinking) to eat. Behaviors such as these, once started, are difficult to erase because of their self-rewarding nature. More about them in Chapter 3, Conversation With a Canine.

Making Training Reliable

The second part of the rewards and reprimands bargain entails making both *reliable*. The dog should not be rewarded for a behavior one day, ignored another and reprimanded another. Remember, you have to think carefully about what rewards the dog might be getting. For example, when a dog barks at the mail carrier, she gets the same reward every time—the mail carrier goes away. Other doggy activities, such as tearing up tissues or going through the trash, are rewards in themselves. These behaviors become habits, since the reward is guaranteed. In creating your own reward system, you have to be just as reliable in the payoff department.

Another crucial piece of knowledge is that dogs pay attention to specifics. If you teach a dog to sit in the kitchen (because you always have a food treat handy!) and practice and practice in the kitchen, don't be surprised if the dog won't sit on command in the living room. If you wear jeans and a loose shirt every day, then one day you're all decked out to deliver a speech to a local service organization, your dog may not sit even in the kitchen. Every variation can be

---

 You Can Quote Me

There is a true epidemic of people who witness several correct responses by their dog, presume learning is accomplished and then hunt around for reasons to explain subsequent wrong responses. . . . In actual fact, a correct response, provided it has been reinforced, is merely like one more grain of sand on a scale: It increases the probability of the same response occurring in the same context in the future. A steady history of reinforcement is necessary to tip the scale in favor of that behavior occurring. It will become highly probable given a sufficient volume of training. . . . If your kid gets 76% on the math quiz, there's no BIG reason. . . . Your kid needs more study. The dog needs more training.

Jean Donaldson, author of *Culture Clash*

Think About It

Kevin was proud that he and his German Shepherd, Trooper, had graduated at the top of their obedience class. Now they were going to show off their skills to everyone at an obedience match. Kevin already had a place picked out on the wall for the ribbon they were sure to win.

There were a lot of people and dogs milling around the park, but it was the same place Kevin brought Trooper every week to run and play, so they were cool. Kevin stepped into the ring with confidence. He was a little surprised that Trooper's on-leash heeling wasn't too sharp. But the big shock came halfway through the off-leash heeling. Trooper shot out of the ring and didn't stop till he'd treed a squirrel at the far side of the park. Kevin slunk out of the ring to go and collect his dog.

Kevin's point of view: He embarrassed me in front of everyone! We practiced and practiced and I know he knows this stuff. I don't know how he could be this spiteful.

Trooper's point of view: The park is for play. Kevin always lets me off leash when we go there, and he tells me to get the squirrels. We don't do that boring walking around in squares stuff in the park. The park is fun!

a distraction for a dog in the learning process. Dogs play by a definite set of rules, but they usually aren't quite the same as ours.

Don't be so quick to assume that the dog has learned something. You may quickly reach a point where, if conditions are favorable—that is, if you're in a location where you do most of your training and there are no distractions in the vicinity and your dog isn't falling asleep—the dog will sit when you say "sit." But try the same thing in a new location or with other dogs (or, worse, squirrels) around or really any sort of distraction, and you may quickly find that "sit" doesn't have the power you thought it did.

The human communicator can also sabotage the learning process. If you get into the habit of repeating yourself ("Sit. I said sit. Sit now. Come on, sit."), you will teach the dog that there is no need to listen until you issue the third or fifth or seventh command. Your first

Think About It

It was my own stupid fault. I thought my Keeshond, Sundance, was right behind me when I crossed the road from the cornfields back to the house. But when I turned to look, she was stopped, sniffing something at the edge of the corn. As she looked up and saw me a distance away, a car came roaring up the hill. Sundance started trotting toward me, and the road, as the car came closer. I don't remember even thinking about it. I just yelled "Down!" I was not a great trainer at the time, but Sundance was a great dog and she had learned English well. She dropped as the car sped on by. I was shaking as I went back to collect her, but she was fine.

command is not a reliable indicator of any consequences. You can also greatly confuse the process by using one word to mean multiple things—"Lie down," "Get down" (off the couch), "Down" (off me). We'll delve further into both of these problems in Chapter 3, Conversation With a Canine.

You can also create problems by issuing commands you don't intend to see through. I call this the "Johnny don't" syndrome. You've almost certainly been witness to the following scenario in some store somewhere: A young child is running through the store, pulling merchandise off shelves or racks, screaming, spitting, whatever. The mother, while continuing her shopping, repeats like a mantra, "Johnny, don't." The words have no effect, but she keeps repeating them nonetheless. This is repeating commands taken to the utmost. It's frustrating for you, for your dog and for everyone in your vicinity.

Think it's kinder not to "insist" that dogs follow commands? Think again. Not only could a reliable command save your dog's life someday (see the example above), but dogs have a social structure based on power and are happiest knowing where they stand in their pack. Confusion is annoying to dogs and to humans.

Our responsibility as dog owners, to paraphrase the song, is to "teach our canines well" and "have a code that you can live by." So you must teach your dog what words mean and that you mean what you say. Your dog is listening, whether you think you're saying anything or not.

WHY YOU SHOULD LISTEN TO YOUR DOG

There is the highly practical view that whatever training you plan to do will proceed more quickly and easily if you can read the way the dog is responding to your efforts. Yet there is so much more to it than that. A one-sided conversation just isn't very interesting. Dogs share so much with us; they're willing to go along with nearly any fool thing we decide we want to do. Although some people may joke about it, they aren't little humans in fur suits—they're much more interesting than that.

Think About It

The Situation: The dog is a perfect angel when people are home. When left home alone, the dog scatters the trash, chews the pillows on the couch and generally ravages the place. When humans return, the dog grovels at the door, sheepishly wagging his tail, sometimes going belly up.

The Human Viewpoint: He never does this stuff when we're around. He waits until we go out and then he does it for spite because we left him home. Look how guilty he looks when we come back. He knows what he did. He should be punished. He's a bad spiteful dog.

The Canine Viewpoint: When my humans leave, I get really nervous and there's nothing to do in the house. Chewing makes me feel better, and I like being close to their smell on the couch. Sometimes there are things in the containers that smell even more like them, so I take those out. I'm so happy to see my humans when they come back, but lately they're always in a growly mood, so I do my best to tell them how much I like them and submit to them. They must go somewhere really bad to be in such a bad temper. But I'll keep trying.

Humans have gotten very good at ignoring their dogs' attempts to communicate.

Karen Overall recognizes that it's easy to think of dogs as small fuzzy humans because we have so many apparent similarities. She ticked them off as follows:

- We both live in extended and extensive family groups.
- We have extended and extensive parental care.
- We nurse before we eat, and eat semi-soft or regurgitated food before we eat solid food.
- We're sexually mature before we're socially mature by a long shot.
- We have social systems based not on threat but on deference and cooperative work.

You Can Quote Me

We think of ourselves as lord and master, and that's a big mistake. All the terms we use—leader of the pack, alpha, the dominant one— more brutality has been committed toward dogs because of those terms than any single set of circumstances, perhaps in the history of mankind. Because we think it's justified. People lie about things they don't think are justified, but in this case we think we're righteous.
Karen Overall, veterinarian, columnist and animal behaviorist

The result of all these similarities is that dogs and humans live in similar group social systems. So it's easy for us to think that everything dogs do is exactly like what we do. It isn't, and thinking it is can lead to serious miscommunication.

One common example is the "he knew what he did because he looked guilty" fallacy. You hear this all the time, often in relation to dogs who destroy things while the owner is away. Check out the box on page 33 to see what's *really* going on.

The dog is so good at reading us; shouldn't we at least try to read the dog? Paying attention to canine communication, much of it non-verbal, not only will help us understand our dogs better, but will also help free us from the language trap. We rely so much on words.

Rather than rushing to label behavior—unavoidably, in human terms—let's make more of an effort to understand it, see it for what it really is. Dogs really don't go around all day scheming about how they're going to take over the pack by walking through doorways before their humans or planning which chair leg they're going to chew the next time the humans go out. They're a lot more reliable than that.

This chapter has been the introduction to working toward effective human-canine communication. In Chapter 3, Conversation With a Canine, and Chapter 4, Seeing Is Hearing, we will learn how to most effectively teach English to our dogs and, in the often-forgotten second part of the communication interchange (communication being a two-way street, after all), how to understand Doglish. Have fun.

Conversation With a Canine

How do you teach English as a second language to a dog?
Why are rewards better than reprimands?

Near this spot
Are deposited the Remains of one
Who possessed Beauty without Vanity,
Strength without Insolence,
Courage without Ferocity,
And all the Virtues of Man without his Vices.
This praise, which would be unmeaning Flattery
If inscribed over human ashes,
Is but a just tribute to the Memory of
BOATSWAIN, a Dog,
Who was born at Newfoundland, May 1803,
And died at Newstead Abbey, Nov. 18, 1808.

Monument to Boatswain, a Newfoundland,
at Newstead Abbey—Lord Byron

The trainer surveyed the puppies and their owners before she stepped forward to begin the orientation. Pint-sized Goldens and Aussies and Labs were sitting quietly with their owners or receiving a few reassuring words and pats. One or two were being fed treats to keep them still. At one side, two women were talking while their puppies, a Poodle and a Jack Russell, jumped up on them, chewed on their leashes or their owners' pants legs and yapped. The trainer really didn't care what the women were discussing, but couldn't help hearing the running litany of "stop that . . . I said stop that . . . sit . . . now sit . . . I told you to sit . . .

quiet" and on and on. As the trainer stepped forward to begin, all she could think of was her all-time favorite movie quote: "What we have here is a failure to communicate."

Contrary to what some people appear to think, dogs do not come into this world with a working understanding of the English language . . . or any other language of human origin, for that matter. You can be as loud and repetitious as you like, but continually yelling "Sit!" at your dog is not going to have the desired effect unless you teach the dog that this sound means he should place his rump on the ground and await further orders. It doesn't matter to the dog if you teach the words "sit," "down" and "come," or "park it," "crash" and "whee." What matters is that you teach the dog something. So, what do you want your dog to learn today?

Don't doubt your dog's ability to learn all sorts of things.

WHAT YOUR DOG HEARS

You may have seen an old "Far Side" cartoon in which a dog sits looking at a woman standing over her. The woman's bubble of conversation says something like "Blah blah blah, Ginger, blah blah blah blah. Ginger, blah blah blah blah blah."

Most trainers realize that dog owners are quick to reprimand a misbehaving dog, but equally as likely to ignore a dog who is doing nothing wrong. The dog, who craves more social contact, gets a very clear message: I get attention from my humans when I (choose one or more of the following) jump up on people, steal underwear from the

Think About It

A trainer who was called in for a private consultation questioned the owner about the dog's background. What she was really interested in, however, was the interaction going on between owner and dog. The owner's answers were often punctuated with asides of "No!" or "No, stop that!" and "No, Bailey!" After several minutes of this, the trainer asked the owner if he thought that Bailey knew his own name. The owner indignantly replied that of course he did. The trainer didn't dispute it, but suggested an experiment. They took the dog out into the yard, and when Bailey had wandered off to sniff the grass, the trainer asked the owner to call the dog's name, nothing more. The owner said, "Bailey," and the dog kept on sniffing. Next the trainer asked the owner to say "no" in a neutral tone of voice. Probably doubting his choice of trainer, the owner complied. At the sound of "no," the dog stopped sniffing and came toward the owner, tentatively wagging his tail. The dog had learned the word that had the most application to his world. Imagine how many dogs named "No!" there must be out there.

Also note that though Bailey's attitude showed he understood "no" to have negative connotations—coming hesitantly with a slow-wagging tail indicates uncertainty of the reception—he still responded by approaching his human. Being a highly social species, dogs find attention and interaction so important that they will seek out even negative attention if it looks like that's all they're going to get.

You Can Quote Me

Decide what you want from the dog immediately. Don't wait till he's six months old to make the rules. Look down the road to see how behavior is going to impact you when the dog weighs four times as much as he does now. Think about everyone he might be in contact with, not just your household.

Mandy Book, author, lecturer and dog trainer

laundry, chew on shoes, beg at the table, bark when I'm in the yard, terrorize the cat. I get ignored when I lie down quietly, sit and wait when my people come home, stand and wait hopefully to be let in. These dogs learn to misbehave in order to get the attention they crave.

In one of the least just circumstances in doggy life, these pets are then labeled "problem" dogs or dogs with "problem" behavior when the owners get fed up with the behaviors they have inadvertently rewarded. Such labels can bear horrifying consequences. In her book *Canine Behavior: A Guide for Veterinarians,* Bonnie Beaver offers the statistic that only 38 percent of dog owners keep their dogs long-term. The rest rehome their dogs, surrender them to shelters or simply turn them loose, often far from home. The single most common stated reason for surrendering a dog is "behavior problems." These "problems" account for up to 70 percent of the dogs euthanized at shelters, a number far greater than dogs lost to all infectious diseases combined. So much suffering and death results from a simple lack of communication and understanding.

Consider what you want your dog to hear from the beginning of your time together. The dog will certainly be listening.

Some people will still tell you that you can't bring a puppy to class till she's six months old. Don't believe it. By then, you've missed one of the most receptive times in your dog's life. Puppies are little sponges, soaking up all there is to know about the basics of the world around them. Yes, there may be some slim chance of communicable disease, but the risk of behavior problems later in life looms much larger.

The humans need the training as much as the puppies. They need to hear things like, "You won't want the dog jumping up like that when he weighs 60 pounds and you're about to leave for work, or your frail grandmother is visiting," so they remember to explain to puppy that feet should be four on the floor. It's not fair to lead the pup to think that jumping on people is great fun and can get you a snuggle or an ear scratch, then suddenly change the message to, "You're a bad dog for doing that"! Start as you mean to finish.

Decide what your rules will be, stick to them and be sure to explain them to the dog (more about that later in this chapter).

Researchers have found that we humans (even the males) often talk to our dogs in the same way that we talk to human infants—with higher pitch, lower volume, shorter phrases, nonsense words. Experts call it "motherese." It's a sign of how close our relationships are with our dogs, and it's perfectly fine for bonding with and confiding in them. As communication with a definitive meaning (other than "I love you"), however, this tone of voice is not very satisfactory, at least for the dog. We may avoid a trip to the psychotherapist by pouring out our hearts to our canines because we can say anything without fear of being ridiculed or criticized. Whatever we confide will go no further, and those big liquid eyes just seem to exude

 You Can Quote Me

Leadership needs to be based on trust and on the dog's confidence in the reliability and constancy of the owner's behavior. Effective communication has no requirement for physical strength, violence or confrontation.

The Waltham Book of Human-Animal Interaction

Think About It

At Wolf Park in Indiana, the researchers have been carefully observing wolves for years. Although the wolves are socialized to humans, they still live in packs and are even given the opportunity to hunt bison. Contrary to relying on such gross signals as alpha rolls and muzzle biting, the researchers have learned to observe how wolves flex the tiny muscles that flare the vibrissae (the whiskers at the sides of the muzzle) to warn another to back off. Canine communication can be highly refined. We'll talk more about nonverbal communication in the next two chapters.

understanding. For the dog trying hard to listen to what we're saying and figure it all out, though, "Muffy, sit" is a lot clearer than "Now Mommy wants Muffy to sit down and listen to the nice trainer." We can help the dog understand what we say by being clearer in our speech.

Our attitudes toward our relations with our dogs could also use some adjustment in many cases. When the hierarchical relationships among wolves first became widely recognized, trainers leaped to adapt them to dealings with dogs. But something went wrong in the translation. We concentrated on *dominance*, seeing power plays in almost everything the dog did. Walking ahead of us on leash suddenly became an attempt to become top dog, and woe to the owner who fed the dog before he sat down to dinner himself. Dogs were regularly thrown onto their backs in what was called the alpha roll. Some trainers even went so far as to advocate biting dogs' ears or muzzles to put them in their places.

Closer observation reveals the fallacy of this line of thought. Lower-ranking wolves grovel or offer their bellies on their own—the alpha doesn't throw them on their backs. In fact, the dominant individual usually appears quite relaxed and unconcerned. Contrary to all this supposed violence, a narrowed eye or flicking ear is

My dog Nestle never seems to miss a word of conversation and excels at latching onto those words he understands.

enough to send a message to subordinates. Some insecure middle-ranking wolves may snarl and tussle, but that's not the behavior of a leader. So what are you *really* telling your dog when you do these things?

As I mentioned previously, thinking of the hierarchy as one of subordinance gives far better results. You, the leader, can then watch for and reward signs of submission (or simply ignore them, as the alpha wolf would, if you have no leadership issues) rather than assigning motives of dominance to everything your pet does that you don't like and punishing the dog for them. It's just what we've been saying—keep it real, relevant and reliable, and start as you mean to finish.

Don't sell your dog's cognitive abilities short. People often want to have some definitive answer about how "smart" their dog is. Trying to compare intelligence across species is a mainly futile exercise—we would fail miserably if our dogs devised some intelligence test based on detecting odors—but if you crave an answer, most experts give the dog credit for intelligence and understanding equivalent to a human two- or three-year-old. Most dogs can learn to understand the meaning of several hundred words and phrases. Some are quite adept at picking them out of conversations, and when owners start spelling certain words, dogs can learn what that means, too.

Ask almost anyone for stories illustrating their dog's intelligence, and you'll usually get at least one, if not many. Researchers discount such anecdotal evidence, but you don't have to. In fact, you can hold the view that it's a good thing dogs aren't any smarter than they are or we'd never be able to stay one step ahead of them. If you find yourself adopting code words for such things as baths and trips to the vet, so "the dog won't hear," you're not alone.

Scientific evidence indicates that most dogs can count to two, with anything more simply classed as "many." If I can put words into dogs' heads for a moment, it might go something like this series: I have one bone. It is in my mouth. I am chewing on my one bone.

I have my bone plus the one I took away from the Cocker Spaniel next door. I have one bone in my mouth and one bone under my paw. I have two bones.

"Many" can create a crisis of possession wherein it becomes difficult to guard all of one's possessions.

I have one bone in my mouth and a bone under each paw. I have many bones.

Considering this counting ability, three toys may be as good as a dozen. The average dog with three toys to choose among will feel she has "many" possessions, and you can keep them fresh and interesting by picking up one set and putting down new ones every few days.

FINDING THE "ONE TRUE WAY"

In the United States, if not the entire technological world, we often seem to be obsessed with finding the magic bullet, an instant solution to any problem, large or small. We're eager to hear the newest expert, follow the next guru. The sad truth is that rarely is any solution easy, let alone instant, and no one ever really knows it all.

Dog trainers are as bad as diet book authors in promoting their own methods as the "one true way" sure to guarantee success, and there are tons of books and videos and special "training devices" available. The dog owner is almost buried under a sea of information and misinformation. How is the average person to choose? Common sense could get you where you need to go, but even that can get lost in the maelstrom, so consider these pointers offered by a variety of experienced dog trainers:

- Any training method should be beneficial to both human and dog. Neither one should find that training makes them frustrated, stressed or angry. While training may be difficult and challenging for either partner at times, it should be enjoyable.

- Never do anything to a dog that you wouldn't want done to you. I know people who have put shock collars on themselves to demonstrate their supposed harmlessness—but they forgot to factor in that they're not giving the dog the same option. If the dog flinches when shocked, the handler says, "See, it's working," not, "Oh, it's too much for that dog. I won't use that again."

- Is the method practical? It's not unusual to feel as if you're all thumbs when starting any new endeavor, but it should get more comfortable with practice. If you continue to feel as if you need three hands, the method's not practical for you.

- Does the person proposing the method have experience in using it with a variety of dogs—big and small, calm and excitable, young and old? Though there's probably a dog out there somewhere that is unsuitable for any given training method, a good method works for the majority of dogs and handlers. If the trainer has only worked with experienced obedience competitors who own Golden Retrievers, that's not a very good field test.

- Does the method or suggestion work for your dog in a reasonable amount of time? Less than a week should produce a change in behavior. If it doesn't, continuing with it is just nagging.

- Does the method allow you and the dog to work together, or is the training done *to* the dog? Jerking up on a choke collar and pushing down on the dog's rump to teach the dog to sit is training done *to* a dog. Rewarding a dog for sitting—all dogs sit, you just have to wait for it—and letting the dog figure out why she is being rewarded is an example of working together.

- Could a child or a senior use the method, or does it require size and physical strength? Do you think a mature woman weighing one hundred pounds is going to have a great deal of success jerking an Akita into "heel" position?

Adopting these suggestions as guiding principles will lead you to what is loosely called positive training. It doesn't completely solve your problem of choice because different forms of positive training exist, but it does narrow the field.

Positive training isn't particularly new. It was popular in the 1920s, but it was buried under the tide of force training when the military

COURTESY OF THE IAMS COMPANY

It really doesn't take much work to make your dog an excellent companion. Invest in your relationship!

You Can Quote Me

It's been estimated that by the time a kid is a couple of years of age, they've had 1,500 times more corrections than rewards. People are raised on that theology, and they haven't gotten a lot of reward in their lives.

Karen Overall, veterinarian, columnist and animal behaviorist

began using dogs and has been slow in returning. It seems strange that such an easy and effective method would lose favor, until you realize the deep-seated problems we humans have with the idea of rewards.

But rewards do work better than reprimands, as you're about to learn firsthand.

THE TRAINING GAME

Developed by Keller Breland, one of the early pioneers of operant conditioning (a type of associative learning in which there is a relationship between the desired response and a planned result, usually a reward), and popularized by Karen Pryor when she began teaching clicker training to dog trainers, the Training Game is a favorite trainer's exercise. It helps people feel some sympathy for what their dogs are going through and why they might be having trouble learning, rather than just expecting the dogs to understand. It also demonstrates the importance of timing.

The game itself is very simple: One person has to "train" another person to perform some designated behavior using only a noise-making device such as a clicker, whistle or squeaker. Just as with dogs, the cue indicates that the subject is doing something reward-worthy. With a dog, you would actually reward each click to reinforce a positive association with the sound, but humans can forego the reward because you can explain that the click means "Hooray, you did it right." In operant conditioning, trainers "shape" behavior. You start by rewarding any action that you think can lead toward the desired behavior, and gradually work toward closer and closer approximations of the behavior. An example may help.

At one of Pryor's seminars, the desired behavior for the first subject was to go to the center of the lecture room and spin in circles. The trainer waited as the subject wandered around the room, and clicked as she neared the center. It only took a few passes before the subject realized that the trainer was telling her something about the location, and marched directly to the center of the room. Once there, the clicks stopped while the trainer waited for the subject to offer more behavior that could be rewarded. The subject tried standing still, setting off in a different direction, even standing on one foot, but nothing received a click. Getting frustrated, the subject turned to look at the trainer—and got clicked. Visibly startled, she duplicated the action and got clicked again. It worked several times, but then the clicks stopped again, the trainer having decided it was time to raise the criteria. The subject stood still, and you could see her concentrating, trying to work it out. Then she turned again, but this time farther than before, and the click immediately came back. That was the breakthrough, and the subject spun in the center of the room, with the seminar attendees cheering and clapping.

There's also the evil twin, the Negative Training Game. In this variation, the trainer can only say "no" when the subject's actions are inappropriate. Desired actions simply receive no response. This is the

---

 ## Try It Yourself

It's time for you to play the game. It's the best way to experience what your communication attempts feel like to your dog.

Get another dog owner to play with you and alternate being the subject and the trainer. Keep the behaviors fairly simple so no one becomes too frustrated. Do at least two rounds in each role.

When you're finished, talk about the experience. Were you receiving enough rewards to keep you happily working at the problem, or did you want to quit in frustration? Most people don't offer enough rewards—something to keep in mind when you're working with your dog.

Try It Yourself

Play this one only under controlled conditions, such as in a class or with others you can trust not to let their tempers fray. The experience can be frustrating in the extreme, both for the subject and for the trainer.

Remember, you're only allowed to say "no." One round will almost certainly be enough to get the point across. Talk about your experiences afterward.

equivalent of training a dog with lots of collar corrections and no praise.

In one round of the Negative Game, the subject quickly moved to a corner of the class area since she received a "no" when she went in every other direction. Once there, she tried touching things within her reach, raising her arms over her head, hopping, but everything received a "no." Any attempt to leave the area was likewise rebuffed. Her efforts became slower and more dispirited until finally she jammed her hands in her pockets and refused to move at all, quitting the game. Under the negative rules, the trainer could do nothing to get her moving again. Only when the trainer was allowed to switch to rewarding with a click could he get the subject moving again. She eventually performed the desired behavior of opening a drawer.

The final training variation contains both rewards and reprimands. Gary Wilkes compares this to the childhood game of "hot/cold." Accomplished trainers agree that this is the most effective way of training, but it's the hardest for novices to master. Many new trainers find themselves clicking when they meant to say "no" and vice versa. Starting with positives only and adding negatives as you become more accomplished may work better for you.

However you play the game, pay attention to what it shows you about the difficulties of interspecies communication. You should end up with a much better appreciation for how much work the dog is putting into learning what you're trying to teach. It isn't as easy as you might have thought.

TEACHING ENGLISH AS A SECOND LANGUAGE USING POSITIVE METHODS

Call it communication or call it training, but if you want to have a fulfilling relationship with your dog, you'd better be doing plenty of it. Once you know how, it's not hard. In fact, unless your canine is a new puppy, you've probably already translated some English, whether you meant to or not. Does your dog leap up at the mention of "cookie" or "dinner"? Does she run to the door if anyone says "go" or "car"? Dogs *will* learn—it may as well be something you want to teach.

The ABCs of Communication

There's no need for choke chains, ear pinches, shock collars or any of the other violent means that have been used as "communication." Remember, we mentioned rewards and reprimands before and tried them out a bit with the Training Game? This simple yes/no switch is the foundation of your personal computer's every activity, so you can see that it's capable of plenty. And you're not even going to ask your dog to construct a spreadsheet or spell-check a term paper!

But the dog does have something the computer doesn't: emotions. So we're going to add a third possibility, a neutral between the yes and no—or, if you prefer, lukewarm between the hot and cold.

Sporting dogs have been around for a very long time; one is featured here on a 19th-century music box.

So first, let's discuss the "yes." That's your reward. For most dogs, the top-of-the-chart rewards include food, play, freedom and praise. You can turn all of them to your advantage, but for your beginning lessons, food will be most useful because you can also use it as a lure to help the dog perform some desired action. The all-important "A" of your communication alphabet is "Any reward." To make the best use of your rewards, you need a keyword to let the dog know her actions are correct and a reward will be coming. So even if you aren't next to the dog, you can still offer encouragement. Some people use words—"good" or "yes" or "right," anything short and snappy—and some use a clicker, a small noisemaking device. The clicker has the advantage of making the same sound each time and not coming up in conversation, but you have to remember to have it with you. Clicker or word, the choice is yours.

Your neutral word lets the dog know that she's not performing the desired action. This is *not* punishment. It's just a clue to help further the dog's training. Trainer Gary Wilkes uses "wrong," but many people find it difficult not to put a negative connotation on this word. If you're one of them, choose something else. Something slightly goofy, such as "nope" or "too bad," will make it hard to sound harsh. Whatever your word happens to be, it's the "B" of your communication alphabet. Think of it as "Better luck next time."

The "C," Consequences, doesn't come into play until later. There can't be any reprimands until the dog knows what the right thing is.

So, once again, it's

A = Any reward

B = Better luck next time

C = Consequences

To start formal communication, you begin with A. Accustom your dog to your positive keyword, so she will know what it means. Click your clicker or say "yes" or whatever word you have chosen, and give the dog a treat. Repeat perhaps a dozen times. Your dog will be delighted! Give it a rest for a while, then have another click and treat session. Make it a point to have your "click sessions" in different locations—you want your dog to understand that any time, anywhere, the click or your keyword means "That's right, and you're about to get a reward!" When the dog begins to "startle" at the sound of your click or keyword, you'll know she's starting to understand.

Try It Yourself

This book isn't a comprehensive training guide, but to show you how your very rudimentary alphabet can work, we'll have you teach your dog what "sit" means. Note that you aren't teaching your dog *to* sit—the dog already knows that perfectly well. You're teaching the dog to sit *on cue*. So, have in your possession:

- One alert, slightly hungry dog
- A pocketful or bowlful of small yummy treats
- A clicker if you're going to use one
- Time and patience

Hold a treat in front of the dog's nose, then move it slowly back over the top of the dog's head. Because of the way dogs are constructed, when the dog's nose moves up to follow the treat, her rump will move down. Voilà! The dog sits, and you never laid a hand on her!

As soon as the dog's rump is on the ground, click or say your keyword, then give the dog the treat. Get the dog up again by playing with her, then lure her back into a sit.

If the dog jumps up to get the treat, you're probably holding it too high. Use your neutral word (the B in your vocabulary) to let the dog know this isn't reward-worthy behavior, and try again, keeping the treat lower.

When the dog folds into a sit as soon as you hold your hand out, you can add the word you want the dog to connect with the action. Say "sit" (or whatever you've chosen), hold your hand out in the same motion but without a treat in it, click or say the keyword when the dog sits and reward. It's that easy.

As Ian Dunbar has pointed out in his columns, a dog that is sitting can't be jumping up on people, running out open doors or getting underfoot. And you've taught the dog a second word.

Puppy's First Word

The very first bit of English your puppy should understand is his or her name. Remember, you don't want a dog named "No!" or "Stop that!" Use your pup's name often and lovingly. (For any of you with purebred dogs with long registered "paper" names such as Shadyoak's Timberland of Twist Water or some such nonsense, the name we mean here is the short one, or call name, you use in everyday conversation with your dog, maybe Twist in this case.) Associate that name with all the good things in life: food, pats, walks, play. In no time, your dog will know that his or her name is a very special sound that has a lot of meaning.

Adding D

Once you start teaching what are commonly called "commands," you need a fourth letter in your communication alphabet. This D, for "dismissed," will let your dog know that the command is no longer in effect. A dog told to "sit" should put that butt on the ground and keep it there until told otherwise, not sit and then immediately pop back up—that would make training pretty useless! So you need a word to negate the command, to free the dog to go about her business. You might even use "free." Other good choices are "take a break" or "off duty." Avoid using "OK." It's too easy for this word to slip out in conversation and free the dog into what could be a hazardous situation.

You can also think of D as "Don't leave the dog under orders."

Dogs are regularly taught to serve as assistants using only positive methods. Terri Nash trained her own dog, Sunny.

Think About It

Only four little letters to remember:

A = Any reward
B = Better luck next time
C = Consequences
D = Dismissed, or Don't leave the dog under orders

With these four rudimentary concepts, you can achieve a high level of communication with your dog and have fun while you're doing it. What could be better?

Some Additional Thoughts

We'll use more hands-on training examples in many of the remaining chapters. But if you want a good book that concentrates on training, check out the Resources appendix for some choices.

Whatever words you choose to teach your dog as commands, they need to mean one thing and one thing only, and they need *always* to mean the same thing. Most dogs can't discriminate between two meanings for one word, and homonyms (different words that sound the same) have only one meaning to a dog. Thus, the word "dear" has left my vocabulary because my dog Nestle hears it as "deer" and reacts with great excitement.

There is some debate regarding how finely dogs can discriminate between speech sounds. Trainers warn against using words that sound too much alike, yet owners who name multiple dogs "Him," "Tim" and "Kim" or "Jack" and "Jock" claim the dogs have no problems responding to their own names and not their housemates'. Until firmer evidence presents itself, it's better to avoid potential problems by using distinctive-sounding keywords.

Once you have taught your dog the *meaning* of a word, your ongoing task is to maintain the *relevance* of that word. Have you ever tried repeating a word to yourself and found that within a dozen or so repetitions the word has lost all meaning and become just so much gibberish? This happens when you talk to dogs as well. Even if you have taught the dog what "sit" means, if you blather it repeatedly without having the dog respond—like the two women in our chapter-opening tale—that meaning will soon vanish. To keep your human-to-canine vocabulary strong, don't just bandy words about. If you say "sit," mean sit, and reward the dog for listening. (Once your dog learns the word, by the way, your reward can be praise or petting or whatever you like—not just food.) Teach the dog that listening to and responding to your communication is always a good idea because it always results in good things for the dog.

And don't be too quick to decide that your dog really understands what you are saying. Dogs are exquisitely fine-tuned to their environment and register changes in circumstances that may seem meaningless to you. So while you may think you have taught, "When I say 'sit,' you put your rump on the ground," what the dog may actually have learned is, "When my boss is in the living room in his clothes that smell like outdoors that I'm allowed to put my feet on, and the strange box in the corner isn't making any sound and the boss makes the sound 'sit,' I am supposed to put my butt on the ground." If the second scenario is true, the dog won't sit if you're dressed in business clothes or the television is on or if you're anywhere but in the living room. This isn't disobedience. This is incomplete learning. Jumping to an assumption of understanding, which then leads to deciding that the dog is willfully disobeying and should be punished, is one of the most common errors dog owners make. Until you have practiced a word in a variety of settings, with good responses everywhere, you cannot truly say the dog knows the meaning of the word. You have to do the generalizing for the dog.

USING NATURALLY POSITIVE AND NEGATIVE SOUNDS

Studies have indicated that certain qualities of sounds contain meanings. For example, all varieties of mammals, from rats to elephants, use low-pitched sounds to send a message to "back off," an implied threat or warning of aggression. High-pitched sounds may indicate the opposite, calling others closer or asking permission to approach, or they could relate to pain. The length of a sound can also matter, with short sharp sounds denoting surprise or a sudden intense reaction, and longer sounds corresponding to more thoughtful, measured responses. Rapid repetition of a sound adds urgency to the message.

We can certainly use these generalities to help us listen to our dogs (as we will in Chapter 6, Canine Spoken Language), but we can also adapt them to our communication with them. In fact, Patricia McConnell, Ph.D., in a lecture at the Association of Pet Dog Trainers annual conference, reported on the signals used by shepherds with working Border Collies, including animal handlers from 19 different language backgrounds. She found that across cultures, in each language, handlers used short repeated whistles or other sounds to increase activity and single drawn-out whistles or notes to slow down or stop activity. To effect an abrupt stop, however, handlers used one abrupt signal.

McConnell also studied several litters of puppies using computer-generated whistles and found that the puppies demonstrated higher activity in response to short repeated notes. Recordings of brain wave activity revealed that puppy brains responded more strongly to the number of repeated sounds than to changes in pitch.

Experimental psychologist and dog trainer Kathy Sdao observed that pitch and speed combine to either animate or inhibit the dog. Loud, high-pitched, fast talking tends to rev dogs up, while slow, lower-pitched tones calm them down. The sharp, staccato sound we use instinctively (for example, "att"), such as when we're trying to signal a toddler not to touch something fragile, often does stop whatever behavior the dog is engaged in at the time.

All of which accords well with the meanings attached to the sounds dogs make, as you'll see in Chapter 6, Canine Spoken Language. There may even be an actual physical reason for these reactions. Within the canine brain (and the human one as well), you'll find the analytical prefrontal cortex (the area of problem solving) and the more primitive limbic system (responsible for emotions). These two areas work in diametric opposition—stimulation of one means inhibition of the other. So a short, sharp sound, often a signal of danger, creates a momentary freeze-up while the limbic system shouts "fear" and the body prepares for fight or flight. By the same token, a dog under the influence of strong emotion is actually physically incapable of clear thought. Is it any wonder that the first night of any dog class is often a noisy, hectic, less-than-rewarding experience? Yet the opposite is also true: A dog engaged in problem solving, such as learning a new exercise, is less likely to fall prey to overwhelming emotions.

Dog owners can use these innate qualities of sounds to their advantage, and can help dogs out in stressful situations by giving them something to do.

THE "JOHNNY DON'T" SYNDROME AND "SPOILED" WORDS

We mentioned this phenomenon before—the parent who issues a continuous stream of repeated instructions at a child, all of which the child ignores. The same problem can occur with dogs.

When you first begin interacting with your dog, your voice is a novel and interesting part of the environment, but the novelty soon wears off. If, by then, you have not begun to teach the dog that your words can have great and attractive meanings, you will have a harder time regaining her attention. Teaching your pup her name and associating it with plenty of positive things, as described earlier, makes a good first step. Simply saying the same word before an enjoyable event—"walk" or "cookie," for example—will soon convince your dog that it's worthwhile to listen to you.

Falling into the "Johnny don't" syndrome, however, will just as quickly devalue words and the dog's interest in them. Don't get me wrong—it's fine to have meaningless conversations with your dog, to murmur sweet nonsense while petting her or to pour out your day's troubles into those sympathetic ears. But words you want to have actual meaning for the dog should *always* have the same meaning.

Many people make a mistake in their choice of a word for instructing the dog to lie down. Over and over, I've heard people tell the dog to get *down* when jumping up, get *down* off the furniture, get *down* when pawing to beg food or attention. These people are astonished when they say "down" and the dog simply stands and looks at them. This problem is so common that I've given up using "down" as any sort of meaningful word. I use "crash" as the verbal signal for my dog to lie down. Anyone who might say "down" to my dog would get no reaction from him.

If you've rendered any words useless this way, replace them. If you're choosing your set of cue words for your dog (a much friendlier way to think of them than commands), consider your choices. Use words you will remember easily and correctly. Go to a beginners' agility class and watch people trying desperately to remember what they've decided to call each of the dozen or so pieces of equipment and you'll have a lively demonstration of the importance of picking easy words. Also, make them words you won't be inclined to use in any other way, so you will keep the meaning pure and relevant. In case you are bereft of alternative ideas, here are some basic choices:

- "Sit" could also be "park," "fold" or "bum."
- "Down" could be my "crash," the German "plotz" or "rest."
- "Come" for my Nestle is "quick," but you could also use "here" or "front."

Note that these are all short, snappy words, easy to spit out. Choose one for each action, —for example, your set might be "sit," "rest" and "front"—and stick to them. Think about your choices before you use them with your dog. Having to change words means having to retrain the dog, an activity you may find frustrating.

Voice Coaching

When speaking to your dog verbally, you can help your communication through several details of voice and approach.

I. Unless your dog is hard of hearing, there's no need to yell. While some dogs (and some people) exhibit selective deafness, pretending not to hear what they don't want to, this is a behavioral issue, not a physical one. Dogs hear more acutely than we do, especially in the higher registers. So if a human friend could hear your normal voice at a certain distance, so can your dog. In fact, whispering often intrigues dogs and may well get you more attention than shouting.

2. Dogs only understand the words you have taught them. The teaching may have been unintentional ("go" comes to mind because we use it for exciting doggy things like "go for a walk" and "go for a ride") or intentional (those obedience commands). But teaching took place. Suddenly telling the dog to "fetch the paper" isn't likely to bring your paper any closer to you.

3. Repeating yourself weakens the message. If you're using the word "down" to mean the dog should assume a prone position, and you say "down . . . down . . . down . . . down" and the dog finally lies down and you say "good dog" and give him a treat, your cue may be, as far as the dog's concerned, "down down down down."

4. Women should make an effort to use a lower, more authoritative voice. Lower sounds (growls, deep barks) display more power and leadership than higher sounds (puppy yaps, panic barks).

5. However, if you're not having problems, there's no need to impersonate a drill sergeant. Would you be more likely to approach someone who sounded like they might beat you up when you got there or someone who seemed to want to party? Put a welcoming smile in your voice.

6. Sometimes it doesn't matter whether the dog understands the words or not. If you need to pour your heart out to someone, the dog is usually a great listener, offering a sympathetic ear and a guarantee that your secrets are safe.

7. Finally, most humans rely too much on words. Sometimes you'll do better if you shut up and pay attention to what you and your dog are saying without words.

THE PLACE FOR PUNISHMENT

The cry "I can't let him get away with it!" rings through dogdom, but we'd all do well to slow down and think about exactly what the dog is "getting away with." Karen Overall points out that dogs are regularly "corrected" for dominant or aggressive behavior, without thought to how ridiculous this might be. Many, possibly most, aggression problems are rooted in fear, so "correcting" the dog for a fearful reaction will simply convince the dog that the feared object (person, dog or thing) really is a threat.

For punishment to be truly merited, the problem must be a real threat to the safety of the dog, people or other dogs, which cannot be allowed to occur under any circumstances. All positive methods of suppressing the behavior must have been tried without success. Only under these circumstances may punishment be appropriate. As Morgan Spector, author and obedience expert, has noted, "people resort to punishment all too quickly as a remedy for a training problem they cannot figure out how to solve otherwise. In almost 100 percent of the cases this puts the burden of the trainer's inadequacies on the dog, and is inherently unfair."

Much of this "he can't get away with it" thinking goes back to the military. We want obedience and we want it now! Never mind that the dog doesn't have a clue what she's supposed to be obeying. Or that we may be asking the near-impossible, as in, "But he doesn't come if I call him when he's chasing a squirrel." I agree with Pamela Reid, Ph.D., reinforcement and learning theory specialist, that if a dog that I had trained chose not to respond to a command, I'd be looking at whether the situation is too different from the one I've trained the dog in. I'd also look to see if there is something more reinforcing in the environment and so on and so forth. And, of course, keep in mind that animals are not machines and you shouldn't expect them to perform with 100 percent reliability.

To sum up, consider these three points when things go wrong:

1. Has the training been thorough, in a variety of locations and circumstances? (Trainers often call this "taking it on the road.")

2. Is the environment too challenging, offering a bigger reward than you can provide?

3. Do *you* get everything right every time? Are you simply asking too much of your dog?

Try It Yourself

The next time you are somewhere safe and want to let your dog off leash, try running through all your basic obedience work first. When you turn the dog free, let her go a step or two and then call her to you in a very upbeat manner. When she comes, give her a really great treat and a pat, tell her how great she is and send her off to investigate again. Whenever she isn't intensely interested in some other activity, call her to you and give her a reward. You are building up your bank of good responses and making it more likely that should you ever really need to call her in, she will respond.

Let's look at those points in order. We've talked a little about generalization before. Dogs don't tend to make great intuitive leaps; they assess each situation. The first point refers to a change in location or circumstances. Even something that may seem insignificant to us means a new situation to the dog, where the old rules may not apply. No one knows precisely how many sets of circumstances you have to work through before a word or a command becomes thoroughly generalized, and even then you may suddenly come up against some new event or object that throws previous learning out the window. You just have to keep reinforcing your meanings positively and consistently.

The most common example of presumed learning (also known as jumping the gun), is letting the dog off leash, then being astonished when she doesn't leap to obey. Usually, the dog has been trained at home in the yard and possibly also at obedience class, nearly always on a leash. The owner, pleased with the results, presumes that's it, training is done. When the dog won't return on cue from running loose on the beach, the owner is infuriated. Has the dog ever been trained on the beach? Probably not. Is the dog being spiteful or showing up the owner? Certainly not. She just has better things to do at the moment.

This is such an important concept. The dog does not merit punishment because the dog is not disobeying. The dog is simply undertrained. The handler is the one at fault. Under such circumstances, Ian Dunbar is fond of instructing, "Take a newspaper, roll it up tightly. Now hit yourself repeatedly in the head with it while saying 'bad trainer, bad trainer!'"

The second point—something more reinforcing in the environment—becomes even worse when the handler is stingy with rewards. Dogs have a great time chasing squirrels or birds or rolling in "stuff." Why should they listen to a bland, unexciting owner, especially if there's an edge to the owner's voice and listening will likely mean an end to the fun?

Pamela Reid recalled a woman that came to her in distress because her dog wouldn't come if he was chasing a squirrel. She thought she was a failure as a trainer, without realizing the high level of reinforcement (chasing squirrels being a very self-rewarding behavior) she was competing against. That was a revelation for her. Once she realized that few people have that level of control over a dog, she relaxed and just managed the situation, not letting the dog off leash where there are highways or other hazards, but accepting squirrel-chasing in safe conditions. She stopped asking the dog to come under such circumstances. You need to look at situations more carefully to avoid putting the dog into circumstances where communication will break down.

Finally, there's the third point: You don't get things right every time without fail. Why should you expect your dog to?

For another look at things to consider before resorting to punishment consult the flow chart in the following figure.

Punishment can also have a wide variety of unintended consequences, and it's difficult to use effectively. Terry Ryan includes this handout on "aversives" (another word for punishment) in all her classes. (This material is copyrighted by Legacy Canine and is used with permission.)

> *Punishment* or *correction* are the terms most people use for doing Nasty Stuff to their dogs in the name of training. The following points will explain why aversives are not usually the path of choice for pet dog trainers.
>
> • Punishment only suppresses behavior.
> • While a dog punished for growling may stop the growling, you may not have changed his feelings toward whatever he's

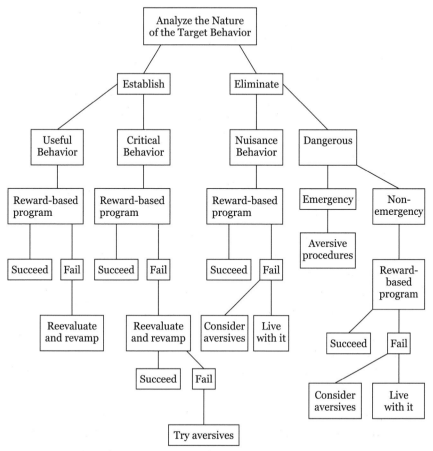

Arriving at punishment slowly and carefully. (This flowchart was designed by Pamela Reid and is used with permission.)

growling at. Because he now feels he can't growl, he may instead bite without warning when facing the same environmental challenge.

- Punishing a fear or anger response can make matters worse.
- Angry or fearful dogs can be made worse. Harsh correction (punishment) can easily escalate the dog's aggression or fear.
- Ineffective attempts at punishment can be a reward.
- The dog stands up and starts walking toward you on the sit stay. You go back to him and place him back into position. He got what he wanted, which is to be with you, for

you to touch him, talk to him, keep him company and not leave him alone. The dog might learn that standing up on the sit stay is a reliable 'Owner Recall Cue'!

- Punishment is an incomplete program.
- Punishment only teaches the dog what *not* to do. The dog might stop the punished behavior, but begin doing something else wrong. An example is a dog who engages in joyous anticipation when the doorbell rings. Instead of punishing an inappropriate behavior like jumping up on people, train and reward an appropriate behavior like "sit" to take the place of the unwanted behavior. Then you can reward at times when you would otherwise be punishing. Doorbell rings and the dog sits quietly on a mat within sight of the door. Dog gets rewarded for sitting nicely by being able to greet the visitor politely, after being released. It is generally easier to instill a behavior you do want than to abolish one you don't.
- Punishment might damage your relationship.
- Earn your dog's attention and compliance, don't demand it. Dog training is about living happily with your dog in society. Punishment often causes confusion and reduces the trust that is so important between you and your dog. It's best to earn your dog's respect by consistency in leadership and lots of good training, not to demand it through intimidation, force or physical abuse.
- Punishment might lead to the wrong conclusion.
- If your dog is pulling on the leash to go investigate or jump on a person passing by and you jerk hard on the leash and scream, "Bad dog," what conclusion might your dog be coming to? Does he think he's bad for pulling on the leash or that the person he wanted to visit is bad? Could this type of training make him worry about people on the street?
- Punishment needs to be consistent.

- Punishment should be administered at the *first* sign of the unwanted behavior and every single time that behavior occurs thereafter. If you miss some of the behaviors and do not punish them, your dog will learn to take his chances and play the lottery.

- Punishment leads to the learned helplessness syndrome.

- The dog shuts down. She decides that nothing she can do is good and so does nothing, just takes the punishment. Doesn't learn, just endures punishment.

- Punishment might not generalize [to other situations]. If your dog is sniffing while you've asked him to heel on leash and you jerk the lead, you are hoping the dog will understand that he shouldn't sniff while in formal heel position. Even if it works as a communication of "no sniff"—and it's always questionable just what the dog is learning—he might interpret it as he shouldn't sniff in that location. It's OK to sniff further along. Or he might learn that he shouldn't sniff on concrete. To sniff on grass is OK.

- Repetitive actions such as barking, digging, chewing and licking serve to calm a dog, much like rocking a baby settles the child. You might be able to interrupt or temporarily stop them, but the dog might engage in substitute behavior even more annoying or dangerous. If you stop a dog from barking, he may begin digging holes, chewing the furniture or licking his paw until it's sore. The calming effect of repetitive behaviors like these is a natural reward for the dog.

- Punishment needs exquisite timing.

- The aversive should be well timed so it appears to the dog to be associated with the specific behavior. That means within a range of two seconds. This is very difficult because you and your dog are not in a sterile environment. It's real life. All kinds of things are happening and the dog might associate something else with the punishment other than what you are targeting.

- Punishment needs to work the first or second time it is applied.
- Your actions are just not having the proper effect if you need to perform them more than once or twice. After that, punishment constitutes abuse.
- Punishment needs to be as severe as necessary.
- The punishment should be aversive and intense enough to stop the behavior right away. The first time! Or you will end up escalating the punishment, until it is much stronger and harsher than if you had started with the appropriate level in the beginning.
- Dogs can think punishment is contingent on the owner's presence. The dog should experience the aversive as independent of the owner's presence, or else you will only get results if the owner is present.
- Punishment should be [used only] to change the dog's behavior.
- The goal of an aversive is to quickly and permanently change the unwanted behavior, not to let the owner feel better because he's "punished" the dog.
- Punishment must be doable by the owner.
- Few owners have the ability and timing, much less the desire, to appropriately select and administer aversive consequences.
- *We have alternatives.*

Now we come to another oft-heard remark: If you only use rewards, you can't be in charge of your dog. This fits well with the whole misapplied "wolf pack/dominance" theory that persists. According to the theory, dogs must be firmly kept in their places because they're continually plotting to overthrow the household. The truth is, the vast majority of dogs are perfectly willing to let someone else be leader. Being the leader is too much work and cuts into their nap time and playtime. If humans fall down on the job of providing leadership, however, dogs may be forced to step in. Dogs that *do* run households have often merely occupied a leadership vacuum. Some owners, in fact, are not even aware that the dog's in charge. (Dogs are often far more benevolent leaders than humans and don't leap to punish *us* at the first sign of miscommunication.)

Karen Overall points out that people who say punishment works may be misinterpreting the results. Let's suppose that you do the alpha roll with your dog (flip her on her back and hold her throat), and she never again commits the doggy sin you were trying to discourage. What you may not notice is that now the dog never again does a whole lot of other normal, unrelated things either because she's so worried that she doesn't dare. If she is a normal dog with no big behavioral problems, you would now assume this dog is wonderfully behaved, when in fact this dog has withdrawn from you. You should want *more* communication, not less.

Overall notes that teachers don't just hand out pens and stacks of paper to eight-year-old humans and wait for them to figure out that they're supposed to write an essay. You would get questions like "Am I supposed to draw a picture?" No. "Am I supposed to make an airplane?" No. "Am I supposed to set this on fire?" No. If the only information you got is what you're not supposed to do, you'd hardly ever learn anything! It's amazing that, even in adversarial relationships, dogs do manage to learn some things.

Long-time positive trainers Bob and Marian Bailey, speaking at an animal training camp, reflected that the staff had only used punishment nine times in more than 100 years worth of training more than 15,000 animals. They've trained gulls to fly miles out over the open ocean and return, cats to sit for hours in busy airports and much more. If they can perform such high-level training using only rewards, you can surely teach your dog to sit, lie down and come.

In fact, the less often you resort to punishment, the more likely it is to be effective and the less severe punishment you will need. Pamela Reid relates that her four-year-old dog, trained without corrections, acted aggressively toward her older dog one day. She grabbed the young dog and pulled him away while giving him a "sound shouting," which the dog found highly aversive and Reid found highly effective, simply because she doesn't use such tactics regularly.

Far better to rely on cooperation, rewarding whatever you find good. Dogs' social systems are close enough to ours to make cooperation relatively easy. If your spouse brings you a morning cup of tea and you reward it with a warm "thank you" and a kiss, you've greatly increased the odds of being on the receiving end of this behavior again. The same goes if your dog remembers to wait at the door instead of rushing into the street and you say, "What a great dog!" and play a rousing game of fetch or chase. It works, and everyone is happy.

Keep this in mind the next time you find yourself leaping toward punishment: If you truly like dogs, you take them on their terms, you make allowances, you have patience and you offer rewards. Some people still ask, "Can I spoil them by using this technique?" I don't think that you can spoil dogs. It's part of our cultural conditioning, with its "you should," "you must" philosophy. We need to let go of it with our dogs. A *need* to dominate companion animals can actually indicate psychological problems. Studies have shown again and again that the most violent criminals—serial murderers, cannibals, torturers—began by harming animals as youths. Relax. Ease up. Enjoy your dog. You'll both be better off.

This chapter has looked at only one facet of communication, using sound. It's the favorite choice of humans, but not of our dogs. We'll look at how we can use body language to talk to our dogs in Chapter 5, Hands Off Handling.

CHAPTER 4

Seeing Is Hearing

Why should you listen to what your dog is saying?
If humans are anthropomorphic, are dogs canomorphic?

> If dogs could talk, perhaps we would find it as hard to get along with them as we do with people.
>
> Karel Capek

From the Mahabharata (an ancient text of the Hindu religion) comes this cautionary tale. A Brahmin king determines to make the difficult celestial journey to heaven. Along the way he loses his family, his friends, finally everyone but his faithful dog. The Brahmin ultimately arrives at the portal to heaven, through which he can see glories unknown to man. Yet Indra, the God of Gods, blocks the way and forbids the dog to enter. With his dog gazing lovingly up at him, the Brahmin cries, "O Wisest One, mighty God Indra, this dog has starved with me, suffered with me, loved me through all! Must I desert him now?" Indra is unmoved, saying, "All the joys of Paradise are yours forever, but you leave here your hound." The Brahmin tries again, pleading, "Can a God be so destitute of pity? Can it be true that to gain such glory I must leave behind all that is left of what I love?" Indra refuses to yield, and finally the Brahmin turns away, saying, "Then I will lose such glory forever. Farewell, Lord Indra. I go and my dog with me." As the Brahmin turns to leave, his dog transforms into Dharma, the God of Justice, who proclaims, "Behold son, you have suffered much! But now, since you would not enter Heaven lest your poor dog be cast away, there is none in paradise shall sit above you. Enter. Justice and Love welcome you."

Now we come to the part that most books leave out: how dogs talk to us. The sad fact is that because dogs are so much better at adapting

You Can Quote Me

Asked what people can do to communicate better with their dogs, Terry Ryan replied, "Learn dog instead of only insisting that they learn human."

Terry Ryan, president of Legacy Canine Behavior and Training

to us than we are at adapting to them, we can often get by without paying much attention to what they're saying. By watching and listening, however, we might avoid some problems, and we'll certainly enjoy a deeper and more fulfilling relationship.

The claim has often been made that language separates humans from other animals. But research such as teaching sign language to primates has eroded this assertion. Again, we have a problem in using the same words for how we communicate compared to how other animals communicate. For lack of a better word, I believe that dogs have language. They communicate through scent, verbally and through an elegant language of gestures. All these types of communication seem to be well understood across the various canine families, from wolves to coyotes to foxes to dogs. Because canines tend to "speak" more with their bodies than their vocal cords, we'll start with body language.

CANINE BODY LANGUAGE

Dogs have remarkably expressive faces and bodies. They combine subtle movements of ears, eyes, mouths, tails and bodies to create a great variety of meanings. A dog's body language may indicate that the distance between individuals should increase or decrease, or impart messages regarding alarm, distress, play, satisfaction, solicitation, identification, affiliation or assembly of the pack.

While some people insist that dogs with drop ears or hair-covered eyes are at a disadvantage in being understood by others, Turid Rugaas, a Norwegian who has spent years studying body language in dogs, disagrees. She notes that dogs take such variations in stride and do not misread the signals of dogs of a different structure.

In general, I think that this is true. Whether my dogs' ears have the half-mast folded position of a Greyhound or the fully dropped and feathered ears of a setter, I can read their ear positions readily, and they don't seem to have problems making their feelings known to other dogs. Still, there are persistent reports that Chow Chows have quite different body language (Chapter 7, Best of Breed, looks at breeds more closely) and that dogs who have suddenly lost a tail through an accident are treated differently by dogs they knew before. So it seems that early learning and socialization play a role, and specific breeds may be better or worse at communicating.

Researchers at the Anthrozoology Institute, University of Southampton in Britain, looked at 10 breeds of dogs to see whether they used any or all of 15 common wolf signals. The breeds, from least to most wolflike, were:

- Cavalier King Charles Spaniel
- Norfolk Terrier
- French Bulldog
- Shetland Sheepdog
- Cocker Spaniel
- Muensterlander
- Labrador Retriever
- German Shepherd
- Golden Retriever
- Siberian Husky

The Huskies exhibited all 15 signals, but the number decreased steadily through the list, with Cavaliers showing only 2 of the most basic wolf signals. Though it appears that certain communication signals may be lost through our manipulation of breeds, it is possible that other signals are being created. Dogs vocalize more than their wild cousins do and wag their tails more. They seem to be more intent on sociability, both within their own species (nearly all dogs permit others to sniff them, whereas only truly subordinate wolves allow themselves to be sniffed) and across species.

Look at this Shiba Inu—what do you think he's saying?

When interpreting canine body language, it's important to read the entire dog. But there's just not room to write about every possible full-body combination of signals, so we'll look at one feature at a time and at some tips on what it may mean when combined with other details. Both humans and dogs place a lot of emphasis on the eyes, so we'll start there.

The Eyes

You're certainly at a disadvantage in reading a dog if her eyes are covered by hair, à la the Old English Sheepdog. Otherwise, keep an eye on her eyes. They will tell you a lot.

When considering canine eye language, staring is of prime importance. Staring is an act of dominance, but not necessarily aggression. Here is our first example of the need to take other body language into account. A dog staring straight at you may be issuing a challenge, but if the stare is accompanied by ears folded back to the head and a "smile" (which we'll differentiate in the section on mouths), the dog is signaling acceptance of your authority by another confident individual (herself). If the dog is staring and smiling, the ears up and the

Think About It

Details mean a lot when you're talking with body language. Close your own eyes and think about this—how wide are your dog's eyes when he or she is relaxed? Are they round, almond-shaped or triangular? How large are the pupils? You can't register changes if you don't know what's normal for your dog.

front part of the body lowered, you're being invited to play. If the dog is a sighthound, staring may mean nothing at all, other than the dog has been bred to use her eyes more than most canines. The dominance stare, with the whole body held erect and stiff, is often enough to settle ranking disputes between canines. If the dog admitting lower rank looks away, the issue is resolved without a fuss. Avoiding eye contact is a voluntary admission of subordinance.

Another often-used eye signal is blinking. This is one of those actions that Turid Rugaas calls "calming signals." Blinking shows friendliness, good intentions and a willingness to get along. Canines will often blink at each other when tense circumstances are being resolved. Think of it as the canine equivalent of a "get out of jail free" card—rather than holding a grudge and continuing to snarl at each other over the same old issue, canines resolve it, then blink to indicate all is forgotten. You will often see dogs blinking at their humans when the humans are being too loud and aggressive or reluctant to get over a problem. Unfortunately, we generally ignore the message.

The extent to which the eyes are opened can also indicate rank. Dominant self-confident dogs open their eyes wide in interactions, while subordinate dogs narrow their eyes into elongated slits. However, remember to consider the entire picture because narrowed eyes accompanied by ears flattened against the head can be an indication of aggression born of desperation, while wide-open eyes may mean nothing more sinister than excitement.

One canine trying to pacify another may close the eyes completely. Steven Lindsay calls this a "cutoff signal," temporarily breaking off sensory contact and giving both individuals a moment to calm down. This signal appears to be motivated by a strong instinct toward self-preservation since it is often returned by the second individual, enabling the two dogs to gracefully avoid a physical altercation.

The pupils of the eyes can also convey information regarding the dog's mental state, but always keep in mind that the amount of light available will also affect how open the pupils will be. Small pupils generally mean a dog is relaxed, even drowsy or bored. When you see pupils grow wider, you're witnessing a dog becoming excited about something. Large pupils signal excitement and a high level of interest in what's going on. But beware if you see the pupils first contract to specks, then expand: You're seeing anger and possibly a prelude to aggression.

Eyebrows can also be informative, and yes, dogs have them. In fact, many dogs have either color markings or hair growth patterns that accentuate the eyebrow area. Interestingly, eyebrow signals mean pretty much the same in canines as they do in humans. Raised eyebrows indicate surprise and eyebrows pulled together over the nose at a sloping angle show anger. Eyebrows that are knitted together and straight downward signal intense concentration, while eyebrows high at the inside and sloping down to the outside show submission or even fright. Dogs have the advantage of being able to erect hair in specific locations, so dominant dogs can accent their eyebrow talk while subordinate dogs can make their eyebrows virtually disappear.

Try It Yourself

Without looking at your dog—keep your head down and doodle in the margins if you have to—draw your dog's eyes when relaxed. You don't have to be Leonardo da Vinci, but try to get the shape and relative size accurate and detail how much pupil shows in relation to the whites of the eyes. Now compare your drawing to your dog. How good was your perception?

Know your dog's eyes; they will have much to tell you.

Eyes and eyebrows expressing submission (left), surprise (center) and anger (right).

The Ears

When it comes to ears, we have greater variation in styles among dogs. Dogs with upright ears are easier for us humans to read, but you can learn to watch the muscles near the base of the ear even in folded or lop-eared breeds. All dogs make the same sorts of movements, but their ears may not look the same. Long, hanging ears don't move as visibly as small prick ears. Long hair on and over the ears makes signals even less clear. Fortunately, the ear signals we most need to read are fairly large and obvious. Even if we miss the finer nuances, we can still communicate.

With the easiest case, upright ears, the ears held high can indicate curiosity, alertness, excitement, dominance, a desire to play or an imminent leap into chase mode. You must also look at the rest of the dog's body language to decide which of these you're seeing. Ears flattened out to the sides, resembling helicopter blades, show uneasiness and uncertainty. Ears drawn back may indicate friendliness, submission, an attempt at pacification or fear. Again, you have to look at the rest of a dog's body language to sort it out. Ears flicking from slightly forward to slightly down or backward signal a dog trying to assess a situation and feeling apprehensive about it. The most ominous ear movement is a sudden shift from upright to a position rotated to the side, but then tucked tightly against the skull. If other body language is in agreement, this dog is protecting his ears before launching a physical attack.

Of course, ear movements may also be nothing more than a dog reacting to sounds in the environment. It takes a bit of time and practice to tell the difference.

Keep in mind that lop-eared dogs can't suddenly prick up those hanging ears when they're interested in something. But you can see the

Lop-eared dogs do have the same ear movements as dogs with prick ears. You just have to watch more carefully to see them.

base of the ear lifting to create a little V shape that isn't usually there. Lop ears *do* move forward and back—it's just not as visually dramatic.

The Mouth

Start talking about canine signals and mention the dog's mouth and a lot of people will think of a snarl. But exposed teeth don't necessarily mean aggression, and many dogs even learn to smile in imitation of their humans. You need to learn to note whether the mouth is open or closed, the tongue lolling out or not and which teeth are exposed. Licking and champing are yet other signals to watch for. The mouth combined with the ears and eyes can provide solid, unmistakable messages.

First, let's consider those oh-so-impressive teeth. Curled lips with a closed mouth, showing few if any teeth, is a sign of annoyance, a sort of "go away, you bother me" comment. Lips curled further to reveal the canine teeth (the fangs) combined with a wrinkling at the top of the nose are a warning to be taken very seriously. This dog is definitely a threat to bite. If you look closely, you'll see that the corners of her mouth are pushed forward. But if the corners of the lips are pulled *back* rather than thrust forward, even though teeth are showing, you could be seeing a canine grin, often used in greeting humans or seeking forgiveness for some transgression.

The natural canine "smile" consists of a slightly open mouth with the tongue protruding a little. A similar mouth position can indicate fear. You have to factor the rest of the dog into the equation to know which you're observing.

Something called "champing," a noisy sucking, chewing motion, harks back to the days when your dog was a puppy suckling at her mother's teats. Champing appears to have a calming effect on canines (and many other mammals) and indicates willing subordinance or pacification.

Licking harkens back to older puppyhood, from the stage just after weaning when puppies lick at the faces of adults to encourage them to regurgitate food. In adult dogs, it's often used as greeting behavior with their humans. This explains why many dogs jump up when greeting people. Licking can also be used as a sign of respect and subordinance. Anxious dogs often lick their lips or the air. Look at a few photographs of dogs and you'll probably see a tongue licking the upper lip in at least one—cameras make dogs nervous.

Yawning can be simply a need for more oxygen, but is also said to be a calming signal and is the one that Turid Rugaas deems most useful for people to use with their dogs. In a tense situation, if you avoid direct eye contact while blinking and yawning, you can send a message to your dog that there's nothing to be concerned about.

To help decide whether a dog is frightened or angry, look to the corners of the mouth. A dog showing teeth in a self-confident angry posture pulls the corners forward and the lips up, showing the canines but not the back teeth. A fearful dog hoping to scare away a threat elongates the corners of the mouth, showing the teeth all the way to the back.

A final small detail of a dog's face is the *vibrissae* or whiskers. Dogs have them above their eyes, at the sides of their muzzles and under their chins. Though the main function of whiskers is to assist the dog in getting around when light is limited and spaces are tight (such as chasing prey down a tunnel), whiskers also factor into body language. When a dog

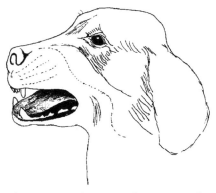

This is a typical version of a canine smile, which could easily be mistaken for a snarl by those who don't know the difference.

is aroused, especially in an aggressive situation, the whiskers stand straight out. In a dog signaling submission, the whiskers are flattened against the head. Dog owners can learn to watch the polka dots where the whiskers come out of the muzzle—when the dots start moving or puffing up, the dog is becoming excited. Dog owners who clip their dog's whiskers (usually for the show ring) are depriving their dogs of these functions.

Face Signals Combined

Learn to put together the signals of the eyes, ears and mouth and you'll be well on your way to understanding canine body language. An alert, relaxed dog has either a closed mouth or a slightly open mouth with the tongue visible, combined with ears erect (if the dog has prick ears) or relaxed at the sides (if she's lop-eared) and eyes neither staring nor flicking away. The entire posture of the dog will also denote goodwill. Many people will smile at a dog displaying this attitude without even realizing they are reading body language.

Even more likely to elicit human smiles is a dog with a relaxed, open mouth combined with blinking eyes, a high tail (more about tail language in a moment) and ears pulled back against the head. This friendly invitation to have some fun is often followed by a variety of play solicitation signals.

Ears pulled back against the head, combined with a mouth showing teeth all the way to the back and wrinkles across the nose and forehead, shows a frightened dog who feels imminent danger of being forced to defend herself. Be careful in reading this one. The same signals minus the wrinkles can be a submissive greeting grin reserved for special humans. You need to know *your* dog to read her signals correctly.

Ears up and forward (even in lop-eared breeds the ears are lifted higher than usual), combined with a snarl showing canines but not back teeth and wrinkles across the muzzle are signs of a challenge by a self-confident dog. This dog is prepared to fight and expects to win.

Finally, ears either flicking forward and back or splayed into helicopter blades, with eyes darting about, enlarged pupils and possibly some lip licking indicates a dog unsure of the situation, trying to decide what stance is appropriate. These signals can quickly shift toward submission or aggression once the dog decides.

The middle figure shows an alert but relaxed dog. Compare this to the bottom figure, a fearful dog who could flee, but will fight if forced to. A "smile" for greeting humans looks similar, minus the wrinkles on the muzzle. The top figure shows a confident, aroused dog who will not hesitate to fight if pushed.

The Tail

Dogs "speak" with their tails through position, movement and even erection of hair. Because we've developed breeds with tail positions ranging from hanging between their legs to curling over their backs, we have to read tail position in the context of what is customary for a particular dog. That's before we even mention dogs whose tails we cut short or even cut off completely. Dogs with only a stub in place of a tail (whether they're born that way or are docked as puppies) lose much of this part of their language, though they can manage a few signals with butt wags and erection of the rump hair. They can compensate with other body signals and generally have no problem making themselves understood. Dogs who lose their tails later in life due to trauma or disease seem to be at a greater communication disadvantage.

Tail wagging as a signal is often misunderstood. You've probably heard someone say that a dog wagging her tail is friendly. This is a hazardous conclusion to jump to because some tail wagging represents a stern—and often last—warning to back off.

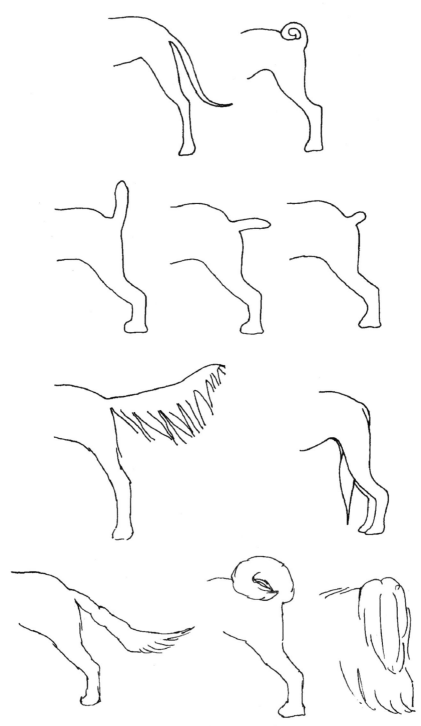

Notice the different tail styles.

If you watch the greeting of dogs who don't know each other, you'll usually see lots of tail talk. Two confident individuals approach with tails held high and wagging fairly slowly at about a third to a half of their full amplitude. This seems to say something like, "I'm willing to be friends if you are, but I can take you on if I have to." After some ritual sniffing, one or both tails will often start to wag more widely and the greeting will change to an invitation to play. Or one tail may start wagging faster, with the dog lowering her body slightly, admitting subordinance to the other dog.

Note that the speed of the wag and the distance it covers both factor into the meaning (combined with tail position, of course). A very wide but slow wag, resembling an angry cat's swishing tail, means you have not found favor with the dog and are being warned off in no uncertain terms. The same wide wag operating at high speed is the excited greeting reserved for a special person or the joyous response to a suggestion of a walk or game of fetch. A very limited but fast wag, perhaps involving only the tip of the tail, indicates tension or stress. But in terriers with tails docked short and carried upright, this small fast wag can mean high excitement. You have to take your dog's structure into account.

Simply looking at your dog will often be enough to generate a small tail wag in response. It seems to be an acknowledgment of social contact, sort of an "I'm fine, how about you?" A broad tail wag at medium speed generally seems to be a sign of pleasure. You can see this behavior during play, as your dog keeps reminding everyone that all the snarling and lunging is meant in good fun. A slow wag with the tail at neutral position or slightly lowered indicates a dog trying to work out a problem. If you see this when you're working with your dog, realize that either you're not making yourself clear or your message hasn't connected with the dog yet. When the dog arrives at a solution (whether it's the one you intended or not), the tail will wag more vigorously. The dog really does appear pleased to have figured it out.

All wags should be read in relation to tail position. In general, the higher your dog holds her tail, the more dominant she feels— although this doesn't work for the Nordic breeds, since their tails are normally carried curled above their backs. Similarly, the lower the tail,

Try It Yourself

Even though you lack a tail, you can imitate some basic tail language. Next time you want your dog to come to you, instead of standing up all stiff and straight, try slouching a bit and wiggling your butt from side to side. Most dogs will read your movement the same as they would read a Doberman or Rottweiler and come bounding toward you to play.

the more submissive the dog feels—although this doesn't work for the sighthounds such as Salukis and Whippets, since their tails normally hang between their legs. In trying to read tail language, you have to remember that all positions are relative to the dog's normal tail carriage. The descriptions I give here use a general retriever sort of carriage, with the tail flowing out behind the dog, horizontal or just below.

The tail held out in its normal position in a relaxed manner is just a carefree sign of interest in the world at large. Should the tail become stiff in this position, however (something that's easy to see but hard to describe), it represents more of a challenge to some other being who has entered the scene. The more the tail rises from this neutral position, the more in charge the dog is declaring herself to be. High tails equate to high perceived rank.

A tail held just a little lower than normal, not at all stiff and maybe swishing gently, indicates a relaxed dog. The dog appears so content that it's just not worth it to hold the tail up that little bit more. As the tail lowers beyond this point, we get into signs of depression, illness or fear. A tail held near the hind legs but not clamped between them could denote insecurity or a dog not feeling quite up to snuff. The tail actually between the legs indicates a frightened dog begging not to be attacked.

Finally, the tail can also bristle. A tail fluffed out along its entire length is an exclamation point accenting any meaning intended by position and wagging. If the tail bristles only at the tip—an area often denoted by a color marking—the dog may be feeling anxious or fearful.

The Body

As used here, "body" includes everything we haven't discussed up to this point, mainly the trunk, legs and paws. As we've discussed in other sections, it's important to read posture and leg movements in relation to what the ears, eyes, mouth and tail are saying.

Invitations to play use a lot of full-body movement. Nearly everyone can recognize a play bow when they see one: front elbows on the ground and butt in the air. There's also the approach-retreat, where one dog rushes toward the other then jumps away, repeated as necessary. Dogs initiating play make a loose and bouncy approach, often swinging their heads and shoulders side to side and making exaggerated movements. Rearing up or standing slightly crouched with one front foot raised can both be invitations to play. Any or all of these signals may be repeated during play, especially if things start to get rough. They assure all involved that no ill will is meant, and normal threat meanings attached to such things as growls, shoulder slams, jumping on someone's back and many more doggy moves are all just fun and games for the present. (We'll learn more about play in Chapter 12, Now We're Talking.)

The body posture of a dog signaling dominance and one signaling submission.

Like tail language, other body language depends mainly on height. A confident, alert dog stands tall, while a dominant dog threatening aggression stands even taller, rising up onto the toes, stretching the head and neck up, bristling the hair over the shoulders and back. Just before the attack rush, the dog will lower the head and ears to protect the throat and ear flaps. At that point, it's too late to do anything but defend yourself.

A lowered body signals subordinance. A confident but subordinate dog will run toward a higher-ranking dog and, when close, slow down and crouch, maybe reaching up to nudge or lick the other dog's muzzle. A less confident subordinate dog will be much more circumspect, lowering the body in a much more exaggerated manner or even rolling onto her back.

Dogs also roll onto their backs and do an odd sort of wiggle dance, rubbing their shoulders back and forth. This has nothing to do with subordinance/dominance. It's a sign of contentment, a sort of celebration that all is well. Face rubbing is another variation. Some dogs use their paws to swipe down their faces from eyes to nose. Our small dog, Diamond (a pound dog, possible a Poodle/Bichon mix), walks up and down the length of a couch, pushing her head and chest against the furniture. You'll often see these behaviors before or after you feed your dog.

A hip nudge was a favorite move of my dear departed dog Serling. The dog walks up to you, turns around and presses against you with a hip or the butt. This is a demonstration of trust and friendship. Similar to our human handshake, which was originally intended to

 Think About It

Do you know your dog's celebration rituals? When you pick up your car keys or pick up the dog's dish to fill it, does your dog leap around in circles, play bow or grab a toy and shake it vigorously? Recognize and enjoy whatever your dog offers—there are few more purely joyful things in this world than a happy dog.

show a hand free of weapons, the dog turns her weapon—the mouth—away.

Serling also used the signal of raising his paw while sitting, usually when I was moving too fast in my training or too keyed-up in the ring. It's both a pacifying gesture and a sign that the dog doesn't understand what you're asking her to do and is starting to feel stressed. Pawing *at* you, however, with the dog putting a paw on your knee, is a sign of friendliness and a bid for attention.

Dog owners everywhere frequently experience the muzzle nudge. It's a friendly but sometimes insistent gesture asking (you might think demanding) attention. Some dogs vary it by resting their head on the owner's knee, somehow making the head progressively heavier.

One dog placing her head over another dog's back, or putting a paw over the second dog's neck, is a show of dominance. Mounting behavior, whether directed at other dogs or at humans, is also an act of dominance. If you are embarrassed by your dog wrapping himself (though females do it, too) around the legs of visitors, you need to do a bit of shuffling of the pack structure in your house.

While we're on the subject of embarrassing behaviors, some owners are mortified by dogs sniffing each other, particularly in the nether regions. If you're one of them, you need to get over it. This is a perfectly normal greeting behavior. Sniffing a pile of poop or where another dog has peed is also normal. If we could get anywhere near the amount of information dogs get from sniffing, we might change the way *we* greet each other.

Urinating, by itself, is a language of sorts. Wolves mark signposts around the edges of their territory. Dogs who find themselves in areas far from their home turf seem to mark more with urine—a sort of "I was here" graffiti. On the same topic, scratching the ground after defecating adds scent information from glands on the bottom of the feet. It is *not* an attempt to cover the excrement. First, have you ever seen a dog actually aim at a pile of poop? Second, dogs *want* other dogs to smell their waste.

In wolf society, only low-ranking individuals allow themselves to be sniffed. Though dogs are freer about sniffing one another, some high-ranking dogs will sit when approached by a higher-ranking dog.

It's a nonaggressive signal meaning "I acknowledge your rank, but we're nearly equal." A similar message is sent when a dog turns her side to another dog, acknowledging the other's higher rank but also asserting her own self-confidence.

Mouthing could indicate a problem with the ranking in your household. Dogs who take their leashes or their owners' hands in their mouths may be asserting dominance. But it could also just indicate that you never taught the dog that it isn't proper to put canine mouths on human flesh, or that you have a retriever who would like to go through life with something, anything, in her mouth.

If you watch dogs in tense situations, you may see examples of displacement activity. Dogs who don't really want to fight but consider themselves equal may break off a staring match to suddenly sniff at a patch of ground, chew on some grass or look at nothing in particular in the distance. They might each urine-mark something, sniff each other's marks and leave it at that. One might suddenly sit down and begin to scratch. Any of these things is telling the other dog, "I'd rather we didn't fight, but I'm not submitting to you either."

These displacement activities occur across nearly all animals. A ranger at Katmai National Park in Alaska told me about surprising a grizzly bear on a narrow path. With this human already inside what the bear considered her personal space (grizzlies have a large personal space), the bear charged the ranger. A few feet short of making contact, she stopped, dropped back onto all four feet and began gnawing at a patch of grass. The ranger backed slowly away and lived to tell the tale. He pointed out that grass isn't a highly desirable food item that a grizzly would normally charge over to eat. The bear had simply let him off the hook.

Turid Rugaas identifies some of these behaviors and related displacement activities as calming signals. Steven Lindsay lists the following as cutoff signals: turning the head away, closing the eyes or looking away, licking, yawning and exaggeratedly slow movements. These behaviors enable individuals to avoid the risk of injury by defusing the situation without fighting. Some dogs also use these messages simply to try to calm another dog. According to Rugaas, humans can use the movements in the same way.

When you begin observing canine body language, you may encounter dogs showing mixed signals. If a dog is staring with wide eyes (dominance) but a lowered body (submission), or standing tall (confidence) while backing away (fear), which signals do you rely on? The safest course with a dog unknown to you is to believe the most dangerous signals. Many fearful dogs will try to escape from or bluff away a threat, but will fight if they feel they must. Even more confident dogs can be conflicted about a situation and reflect their indecision in their body language.

CHAPTER 5

Hands-Off Handling

Why should you rely on more than a leash and your voice?
How do dogs know what we're about to do?

> The dog has seldom been successful in pulling man up to
> its level of sagacity, but man has frequently dragged the dog
> down to his.
>
> James Thurber

*In the ethos of Gnosticism, it is said that the demiurge (a deity, but not the
supreme deity) wanted a center for the universe being created by the supreme
being. So on the fourth day of creation, he made the dog the center of the universe. But while the demiurge saw the dog as the center of the universe, he
expected the dog to be humble. Instead, the dog shared the view that he was
indeed center of all. So the demiurge decided the dog must be punished. After
some thought, he hit on the idea of making the dog the servant of a race that was
inferior but firmly believed that it was the center of the universe. And so the dog
came to live with humans.*

Have you taken to heart yet the idea that body language is the primary language of dogs? We're going to put that concept into action
in this chapter by learning how to use our own body language to help
in communicating.

Having a nonverbal way to communicate with your dog can come
in handy in so many ways. Dogs learn body language more quickly
and easily than spoken language. You can "talk" to your dog while
you're speaking verbally to someone else (dogs love to act up while
their humans are on the phone) or where there's too much noise or

distance between the two of you for her to easily hear you. And, looking down the road to your time with an elderly dog, you will still be able to communicate if your dog goes deaf.

So don't delay—start using the "silent language" with your dog today.

USING BODY LANGUAGE TO HELP YOUR DOG LEARN

First things first: You can't visually communicate with your dog if she isn't watching you. An exciting owner who might announce a walk, launch an impromptu training session or initiate a game at any second will find seemingly fast-asleep dogs suddenly alert to any promising movement. Humans who keep their dogs out in the yard all day deny the dog interaction with them, and humans who don't do much more than put down a bowl of food once or twice a day don't merit much attention.

So, let's be honest here—are you an interesting owner or not?

If you seem to have the dog's attention most of the time, you can use that to your advantage. I keep a small jar of treats next to my chair, and by simply lifting the lid of the jar I can immediately have a dog in front of me, eager for a lesson. Because the lesson can be given entirely with hand signals, we don't even disturb anyone watching television!

You can use body language to good effect in teaching new behaviors. When you move a food lure to mold a dog into a sit or down, the dog watches the treat *and* the hand holding the treat. The motion you make to lure the dog (or some more refined version of it) usually

 You Can Quote Me

Dogs are postural creatures, tuned into the world of body language. . . . Our dogs are always 'reading' us and place a higher value on our body language than the words we speak.
deafdogs.org, Web site for owners of deaf dogs

Try It Yourself

All right, you're sitting down somewhere reading this book. If your dog is in the room with you, or somewhere within earshot, read to the end of the sidebar, then try this out.

Close the book and look up. Is your dog paying heed to your actions? It might be only an ear flicked in your direction, or a whole wagging body suddenly materializing in front of your chair.

No reaction? Try getting up out of the chair. What's the dog doing now? Is there any reaction to this move? If yes, you can be pretty sure that your dog is paying attention to your movements most of the time. If no, it might mean you need to become a more interesting owner, or that you're reading this book at a time or location in which the dog knows nothing exciting is likely to happen (in bed, maybe). You decide.

becomes the hand signal for the behavior. Many people, eager to use verbal language, also give a spoken command at the same time. However, odds are good that if they were to stand still and just say the command word with no accompanying hand motion, the dog wouldn't respond. Trying it the other way around, using a hand signal but no verbal cue, usually works.

Some trainers will caution owners not to "put a command" on a new behavior you're working on because you want the command to mean the *final* behavior, after you've smoothed off all the rough edges. What they generally mean is don't use a verbal command while you're still in the process of shaping the behavior. But you are probably cuing the dog with body language while you are working on the behavior, even if you don't realize it.

Understanding that what your body is saying is more important than what your mouth is saying should help keep you from shouting unheeded commands. Knowing ahead of time what you want your hand signal to be can also help make sure you are clear while you develop it. Some people have used signs from American Sign Language, which dogs can learn to read just fine, though some of the gestures are too small to be visible at a distance. Others use what have become somewhat standard signals, such as a palm up with hand moving upward for "sit," palm down with hand moving downward for "down," arm held straight out to the side then bent at the elbow to bring the hand to the chest for "come." It doesn't really matter what your signals are, as long as you are consistent in their use and your dog can see them clearly.

Once you and your dog have been working on silent training for a while, you will find that your body movements can really influence what your dog is doing. Shifting your weight visibly to one side will produce the same movement in your dog—a useful phenomenon if you want a behavior performed with one paw rather than the other. Trick trainers can teach a dog to wave with either paw by shifting their weight so that the dog is leaning on the paw they don't want used, then signaling with the hand closer to the paw they want her to wave. The same technique can get a dog lying sphinx-style to roll onto one hip or the other. All without a single word or any physical contact.

This is Magic, once the spokesdog for Old Navy. Magic is a well-paid canine performer who responds to dozens of hand signals.

You Can Quote Me

Hand signals may be easier for a dog to learn, and there are probably two reasons. One, dogs are physical animals attuned to reading and responding to body language. Two, we humans talk so much that our verbal cues can get lost in the babble.

Morgan Spector, author and clicker training specialist

DIFFERENT IN SOME WAYS, SIMILAR IN OTHERS

The behaviorist Patricia McConnell finds that many of our modes of communication are closely related to those of our cousins the chimpanzees. We both reach our hands toward things of interest, repeat the same sound over and over and louder and louder when excited, are more aware of vocal communication than visual signals and get dramatic and sometimes violent when frustrated. This is not a good fit for communicating with dogs, who hear and see all of these cues as somewhat alarming and even threatening. Dogs use visual signals more than vocal ones and concentrate on defusing situations rather than escalating them.

Dr. Roger Abrantes delved into human-to-human communication and found that we aren't so different from our dogs after all. Abrantes has noted that in human-to-human conversation, "The verbal part—words—accounts for 7 percent [of human conversation]. The vocal part—tone, dialect, accent—for 38 percent. And the nonverbal part—body language—is 55 percent." This explains why some people find telephone conversations so unfulfilling—much of the communication component is missing.

Humans and canines both have areas of personal space, which they try to influence through body language. If someone comes too close, invading our personal space, both humans and dogs retreat if given the chance. When retreat is not an option, we fidget. Humans might rock, tap with their fingers or swing their legs. Dogs might shift their feet, flick their ears, blink or lick their lips. If the situation doesn't improve, humans often hunch their shoulders, tuck their chins to one shoulder and close their eyes. In the worst cases, aggression may follow. Dogs may lower their heads and turn toward the side, stop blinking and narrow their eyes to slits while the hair rises over their shoulders. Aggression may follow. Neither case should be considered unexpected or unprovoked. Both species gave their best warning signals.

DEVELOPING ATTENTION

After conducting the attention experiment in the Try It Yourself box on page 90, if you found that your dog isn't watching you that intently, you'll need to work on gaining her attention before you can expect to use signals most effectively. Do keep in mind that dogs don't have to be looking straight at you to be watching intently because their visual field is far wider than ours. Eye shape and placement as well as head shape cause some variations across breeds, but most canines can see a sweeping 240 to 250 degrees, meaning they can see behind themselves to some extent. A good human field of vision is 180 degrees, pretty much straight out to either side.

So realize your dog may be watching even when you think she's not. To be sure she is, you can pull surprises out of your hat occasionally. Keep a handful of kibble in your pocket and suddenly throw a few pieces around the room, for example. (Dogs are engineered to hunt for food, and even hunting in the living room is more exciting

Think About It

You may not be fully aware of how much you and your dog are relying on signals. When you tell the dog to lie down, do you keep your body still, or do you automatically bend over and motion toward the floor with one hand? Try holding your body still while giving your cue word (in a conversational tone, please, not a "death to dogs who disobey" verbal scowl). Does your dog seem confused? Does she even perform the desired action at all? You both may need body language more than you know.

You Can Quote Me

Social signaling in the wolf and dog entails very subtle visual cues, produced, for example, by lip and ear movements. Although we cannot produce the same types of movement, if we are consistent, dogs soon learn how to "read" human body language, our nonverbal communication. As dogs are predators, they have a good ability to detect minute movements and thus are perhaps better at reading human movements than we are ourselves.

The Waltham Book of Human-Animal Interaction

than walking up to the food bowl.) Or whip out that tug toy and initiate a rousing game of tug-of-war.

This is *not* the level of attention that some obedience competitors demand, where the dog has to be staring into your eyes. This is just an awareness that it's worth it for your dog to keep at least the corner of one eye on you for unexpected good fortune.

One trick I use with my dog Nestle is to deliver a hand signal with no prior warning. If he complies, he gets a really great reward. If he misses the signal because he wasn't watching, I say "too bad" (that's *my* B, "Better luck next time"—remember your ABCs from Chapter 3, Conversation With a Canine) and he knows he missed something.

USING YOUR BODY TO TALK TO YOUR DOG

You can enhance your relationship with your dog, put more power behind your commands and even avert potential disaster through body language alone.

To take the last example first, several dog experts have spoken about stray dogs in the middle of busy roadways. They could have tried to yell commands over the rush of traffic, but of course they had no idea what words the dog might know. Instead, they used body language. When they needed the dog to stay still to avoid being crushed under the wheels of speeding vehicles, they stood tall and faced the dog directly. When there was a break in the traffic and they could urge the dog closer to safety, they turned sideways to the dog, bent over slightly and moved a step or two away from the road. In each case, the dog froze when faced directly and moved forward when the person turned and moved away. All the dogs made it safely to the side of the road, all because of this little dance of body language.

When I was handling a dog in animal acting, I was suddenly required to have the dog move forward hesitantly. It wasn't something we'd trained in advance, but that's a common occurrence in the world of commercials and movies. Trainers need to know how to get things done with a minimum of fuss, usually with someone yelling "Time is money." This was an easy one. With the dog in position on his starting mark and me out of camera range, I faced him really directly, scowled at him and gave him a very small "come" signal. He took a few steps forward, unsure what I was telling him. To keep him moving, I turned my shoulders slightly away and smiled, then put on the brakes by facing him and scowling again. The effect was quite dramatic; we got it in one take and everyone was happy—even the dog, who got half a sandwich from the catering trucks as his reward once the sequence was over.

In group classes, we see handlers contradicting themselves with their bodies all the time. Someone will be asking a dog to move from

---

Think About It

How did you learn to call your dog to you? Most classes use the formal obedience competition recall, with the owner standing tall and facing the dog. But if you're not competing, why should you handicap yourself like this? Turn sideways, crouch down a bit, even take a step away. Use your voice *and* your body to tell the dog you want her to come close. If your dog should ever get loose out in the open, you'll be much more likely to bring the dog to you by running away than by chasing after the dog. Most dogs love to play keep-away, but will come running to see where you're going if you let *them* do the chasing.

a down position to a sit while bending over the dog in a posture that signals the dog to stay down. When the person is told to stand up straight, the dog suddenly responds to the sit cue. Some people stand slumped over as if they're asking a miserly boss for a raise and they compound the problem by using a wheedling tone of voice. Their dogs often ignore them. Once they learn to be a bit more authoritative (which doesn't mean shouting commands or becoming a drill sergeant; it just means appearing more confident and in charge), their dogs usually start to comply more readily.

In the fast-moving sport of agility (an obstacle course for dogs, with jumps, tunnels and other obstacles that dogs must negotiate quickly and correctly in a different pattern every time), handlers know that body language is critical. Casting your glance the wrong way, turning your shoulders ever so slightly, even bending over just a bit and sticking out your butt, can all send the dog off course. People yell plenty of commands when running the course, but the cues vary in importance. Directional commands are most useful ("go" to keep moving straight ahead, "out" to move away from the handler, "left" and "right" to turn). Agility dogs often just ignore commands that don't agree with the handler's body language. For example, new handlers often confuse their commands when running, saying "walk" (for the dog walk) when they actually mean "climb" (for the A-frame). The dog nearly always ignores the verbal "walk" and climbs the A-frame because that's what the handler's body is indicating.

 You Can Quote Me

If you are herding sheep or working as an animal control officer, your body language is pretty important. If you are a pet owner, the types of body cues you are likely to give are less functional but more appropriate. It is good for the average dog owner to know that getting down low to the ground is a non-threatening posture. When a dog escapes or slips its leash, sitting on the ground is far more likely to get the dog to return than stomping around bipedally.

Gary Wilkes, columnist and founder of Click & Treat

You Can Quote Me

They are so skilled in communication, dogs and wolves. They just make a little grin and a sound and the other keeps away. We yell at them for the same thing. We need to learn to respect them.

Turid Rugaas

BODY LANGUAGE TOUCHES THE MIND

Dogs don't lie with their bodies. (Most humans don't either, if you know how to read the subtle signs.) A dog with loose, easy movement, her tongue flopping out of a smiling mouth, her tail relaxed and wagging, is not hard to read as an outgoing, friendly representative of the canine race. Likewise, a stiff-legged, staring dog with head lowered and teeth bared is definitely not inviting you to rush up for a face lick.

While no one would advise trying to get a snarling dog to lie down and roll over, in less extreme circumstances you can influence the dog's mind by changing her body. Dog experts ranging from Linda Tellington-Jones (originator of a very special type of animal massage work called Ttouch; you'll read more about this in Chapter 8, A Touching Experience) to Suzanne Clothier recommend helping nervous dogs adopt a more confident posture by gently raising their heads and tails. Ian Dunbar advocates teaching dogs to roll over and expose their bellies as a completely nonthreatening greeting.

Owners can also use the dog's own calming signals to communicate the message to relax. Turid Rugaas says that the most useful signals for humans to use—the ones most likely to translate correctly across species—are stretching, blinking and yawning. Try them sometime when the situation is starting to get tense and see if you can change a canine mind.

SPECIAL USES FOR HAND SIGNALS AND BODY LANGUAGE

Dogs can go deaf from trauma or from a variety of diseases and certainly as a result of old age. If you have regularly used hand signals throughout your dog's life, your communication can continue nearly intact. I first learned this with Serling, who was the first dog I ever had who went deaf. Because he had been my performance dog, in every meaning of that word, we used a great many signals. So even under these changed circumstances, we were able to continue to communicate just as well, except that after his hearing loss, he had to look back to see which way I wanted him to go when running ahead on a trail, rather than listening to me yell "left" and "right."

Hand signals and other visual cues made up our repertoire. Serling went on pet therapy visits, entertained groups of children and competed in talent contests. He amazed people with his ability to bark out the answers to math problems because our cues became very subtle, in some cases down to the movement of one finger or even a shift of my eyes. Though I would never say Serling wasn't an exceptional dog (as have been all my other dogs), this isn't particularly astonishing training. It takes practice and a dog who pays attention. But you too could have a doggie math whiz, if you so desire. Just gradually make your signals smaller. Turn your body slightly, use the

Many senior dogs become hard of hearing.

COURTESY OF THE IAMS COMPANY

hand away from your audience and be ready to cover any mistakes with some clever patter. One troublemaker once gave Serling a problem that worked out to zero. I was a little concerned because when I turned to him and stated the problem and then stopped, that was usually enough to start Serling barking his answer. So I scowled in a look of deep concentration on this difficult problem and that was enough to let Serling know something was different. His response was to mumble rather than bark, which I interpreted for the audience as a complaint about trick questions. It went over just fine.

Of course there are more utilitarian uses for signals. Remember all those dogs who bark when the owner is on the phone? Keep a jar of treats near your phone and you can practice all your commands while you have an uninterrupted conversation. A double use of time!

I find that I use hand signals almost without thinking at times. My house features a narrow floor-to-ceiling window next to the front door, so the arrival of any delivery person or guest engenders great excitement. Nestle is allowed to alert me to the fact that someone has arrived, then be quiet when I say, "Thank you." He can manage the quiet part until the delivery person actually touches the little front porch. So I sometimes move to the door of my office, only a few feet from the front door, and start giving hand signals. Nestle then has to divide his attention between me and the arriving package, and can usually be quiet.

 You Can Quote Me

Use signals that are clear, concise, consistent and well timed. Don't ramble in long sentences, expecting your dog to decipher your meaning. Take the anger out of your voice. Remember that dogs are sort of like "aliens among us." They aren't little four-legged furry people. Their brains work differently than ours. They don't do things out of spite, nor are they motivated by guilt. Also, they live in the present moment. The past and the future are pretty irrelevant, so focus on communicating to them about their behavior at the present moment.
Kathy Sdao, animal trainer and behavior specialist

By training your dog to respond to hand signals, you don't have to interrupt your conversation with arriving guests to ask the dog to sit for greetings. Because this results in less stress and frustration, everyone stays in a better mood and the visit is more enjoyable for all concerned.

HUMAN BODY LANGUAGE THAT DOESN'T SUIT THE DOG

We humans often do things with our hands and bodies that actually violate the conventions of dog society. The fact that we usually get away with it is another testament to how tolerant most dogs are of our sometimes strange (to them) behavior.

Reaching out and patting a dog you do not know on the top of the head is highly impolite and inappropriate. In fact, the researchers at Wolf Park have learned they can make the wolves stop pestering them for attention by patting the wolf on the top of the head. Yet if the dog grumbles about this untoward human behavior, the blame gets placed on the dog! Far better to understand what we are doing, and to learn better interspecies behavior. When greeting dogs, the proper etiquette is to hold your hand out for the dog to sniff. If the dog appears particularly shy or nervous, you can crouch down with your side facing the dog and hold your hand slightly out from your body. After the dog sniffs your hand, you may try petting under the chin or on the chest. Reaching over the head remains inappropriate unless you know a dog well.

Hugging is another human behavior that doesn't suit dogs well. Being restrained constitutes cause for concern in the world of dogs, and either reaching over to hug from the side or going intimately face to face to hug front to front are not acceptable canine etiquette. Yet we like to hug our pets—it makes us feel good. Most dogs can learn to accept hugging from their people. Just don't do it with dogs you don't know.

Dogs and humans don't view what we would call kissing in quite the same way either. In the canine realm, subordinate dogs lick the side of the mouth as an appeasing greeting to higher-ranking individuals. Many will try to do the same thing with their humans. Some people don't like it, but it's a sign of respect for your leadership.

Well, maybe they don't look alike, but they sure are interested in the same thing.

Humans kissing dogs is another matter. Some people do smack their dogs right on the lips. Dogs may misread this gesture as a statement of subordinance. Kissing the dog on the top of her furry little head avoids both that misinterpretation and direct eye contact. If you do kiss your dog on the face, be sure the dog will welcome, or at least tolerate, such close contact before bringing your face so close to the dog's main weapon, her mouth.

By the way, if you're wondering about the hygienic aspects of your dog licking you, the chance of any disease transmission is very low. Humans and dogs don't share many bacterial or viral infections. A slightly more probable scenario is a dog who has internal parasites such as roundworms, who licks herself and then licks you. But this is still an unlikely situation.

Looming over translates as a mild threat in canine language.

People also tend to loom over their dogs. For example, an owner might reach over his dog's body to untangle the leash from her leg. In canine society, putting your leg over the back of another or resting your chin on the back of another individual's neck are signs of dominance. Leaning over your dog can make her nervous. It's better to reach under her body or maneuver around to her other side instead.

Learning to "think like a dog," at least a bit, can certainly smooth out human-canine relations. If you get really good at it, you can have a bond more profound than you ever imagined. Giving a canine signal that fits the situation—even something as inconsequential as stretching when you get up from a chair—can start your dog looking at you in a whole new way.

CHAPTER 6

Canine Spoken Language

Do dogs really mean things when they make all that noise?
Do dogs from different countries understand each other?

When the old dog barks, it is time to look out.
Beware of a silent dog and still water.

Latin proverbs

Dogs have had symbolic meanings throughout history. In the East, they often stood for the concepts of vigilance and protection. Statues of dogs of various sorts guard the entrances to many Asian temples and tombs. In the West, they more often represented loyalty and fidelity. Tomb effigies in Great Britain often include a dog lying at the feet of a deceased master.

The dog has a firm place in astrology. When Buddha gathered the animals and honored some with their own year, the dog was one of the 12 species chosen. So in the Chinese calendar, every 12th year is the Year of the Dog. The Mayans and the Aztecs both included the dog in their calendars, with the 10th day of a month symbolized by a canine. It was considered a lucky day to be born, conferring powers of leadership.

Now we come to the secondary form of canine language, vocalization. Yes, I know that some of you will say your dogs vocalize all the time, but sound is not necessarily the same thing as communication. Dogs who bark or whine when left alone are more likely consoling themselves than saying anything.

Vocalizations are hard to describe in print. We humans don't even agree on what the basic sound is that dogs make. In English-speaking countries, it might be described as "bow wow" or "woof" or "arf."

This is my dog Serling. He had just won a talent competition at the county fair, and he was intent on telling the world about it. The photographer caught him mid-bark.

Other human languages come up with different interpretations, such as "wung wung" in Chinese or "jau jau" in Spanish.

Dogs are limited in the sounds they can make by their anatomy. They don't have the complex voice box that humans do, and their airways are designed to maximize breathing and smelling while running, not to speak. Their mouths, lips and tongues aren't highly mobile. Though there is the occasional dog who learns to imitate a human word or two ("mama" and "I wuv you" are popular), that's about as far as they can go in speaking our language.

Understanding our language is another matter entirely. Dogs can comprehend several hundred words if their humans take the time to teach them.

I will try to break down canine vocalizations into categories and examine each one in detail, but realize that some categories overlap and some dogs combine sounds into "sentences." For this section, I wish this was an audio book. I'll do the best I can.

BARKS

Everybody has heard dogs bark. But have you stopped to think what the barking *means*? Can you differentiate different barks your dog makes?

Barks can mean a great many things. They might be an alarm (and different objects can elicit different alarms), a greeting, an invitation to play, a call for companionship, a cry of distress, a warning or threat, a sign of excitement, a request for care, a tool while herding or hunting or simply a group shout. It helps to be able to observe the

 You Can Quote Me

Her bark as I'm leaving the house ("take me with you") sounds much different than her bark when greeting a doggie friend ("I have a toy, want to play?"). These both sound different than the barks that seem to mean "I'm overtired" or "hurry up with my dinner!"
Kathy Sdao, animal trainer and behavior specialist

Try It Yourself

Go out of the house and stay within hearing distance. Listen, and if your dog is anxious about being left alone, you'll hear a single bark, a pause, another single bark, another pause and on and on. The barks are high in pitch and sound sort of frantic. Other dogs, who aren't really suffering separation anxiety but are bored when left alone, also give a single bark then a pause, but the barks are mid-range and have a strange dampened quality. They don't seem to have any real emotion or meaning behind them, and if we could ask the dog, we might find that they actually *don't* mean anything; the dog is simply trying to pass the time alone. The truly anxious dog doesn't know how to make herself feel better, and just keeps telling the world at large "I'm lonely, please come back."

dog doing the barking because body language will conform to the message in the bark.

In dogs, barking starts as early as three weeks of age. Wolves rarely bark, and when they do, it's a surprisingly soft and almost always single "wuff," generally used to challenge an intruder. In our long relationship with canines, we seem to have selected hearing (conscious or unconscious) for barking. Is it any wonder that in a recent survey, two of the most frequently reported problem behaviors were barking and growling?

Of course you don't want your dog barking at all sorts of inappropriate times, but you should pay attention to those barks. You'll be surprised how much you can learn to understand.

Dogs vary the pitch, length and number of their barks, as well as the time between them. Dogs can even vary the "word" of their bark. For example, you may think your dog normally says "woof," but she might, on some occasions, say "arf" instead. I'll try to describe some general barks and their meanings, but keep in mind that dogs are individuals and you'll have to adjust these descriptions to your own dog's communication efforts.

One bark results from separation anxiety. You'll know this is happening when you start getting calls from your neighbors because the barking starts after you leave. If you have a separation anxiety problem, see Chapter 11, Solutions to Common Problems, for advice on how to accustom the dog to being left alone.

Other barks are mainly various forms of alerts. We have developed dogs to guard the homestead and flocks, after all, so we shouldn't be surprised when they do their job.

Some dogs are very easily stimulated and will bark at almost any movement they see. The barking is high-pitched, without a lot of pauses, and the dog usually jumps around while barking. These dogs need to be taught to control themselves. Some good obedience training will teach the dog to focus on you and be rewarded for sits and downs rather than getting into a shouting match. Because these dogs are active and observant, once you get their attention, they are generally very good at lessons and a joy to train. To them, barking at things is fun and exciting, so you need to provide other outlets for their enthusiasm.

Letting your dog alert to strangers arriving on the scene probably isn't a bad idea. But you should be able to stop the noise after a few barks. You will have a much more effective warning system if you can extract greater meaning from those few barks.

Your dog's initial alert may consist of three or four quick barks, neither high nor low, and then quiet. She has noted something in the environment and is calling it to the attention of her pack (you). The dog will be oriented toward the source of the intrusion. If the intruder approaches, or the dog feels the situation could be changing to more of a threat, the barking will become more continuous. If at some point the dog feels that a definite threat is coming close, the barking will continue at a lower pitch with slower repetition with the barks themselves more drawn out.

If you know that your dog is alerting you to the (presumably) innocent presence of the UPS truck or the mail carrier, you can cut the barking short by telling the dog "thank you" and offering her a really scrumptious treat. If the dog is reluctant to give up the alert, turn on the radio to mask the sound of the truck and move the dog away from the window. For these more insistent dogs, clicker training can work really well in convincing them to come to you for a reward after you've said your "thank you" and expect them to stop barking.

In a nutshell, clicker training means you use a little noisemaker (the clicker) as a marker for desirable behavior. You follow the click with a treat, so the dog knows that the click means a treat is coming. The association becomes quite powerful, and if you click for the dog being quiet (even if it's only for a second at first), you can work up to longer silence, and ultimately to the dog alerting and then coming to you for a reward. There are plenty of books out there that explain clicker training, including one of mine (see the Resources section for more information; Chapter 3, Conversation With a Canine, also presents some information on the subject).

Some dogs bark not to alert you to anything, but just to get attention. Dogs quickly learn that barking will often cause a person to appear and bark back (our yelling pretty much equates to their barking). While you may not think being yelled at is an enjoyable thing, to a dog it's better than being ignored. Yelling at a dog barking for attention is actually providing the reward the dog is seeking!

A bark for attention usually has a higher pitch. Often, the dog will bark once, then pause to see if there's any response. If you are in visual contact with the dog, the pause may include much tail wagging, circling or even a play bow. The dog will do whatever it takes to get your attention. These dogs are usually bright, charming individuals, and you could gain much by interacting more with them. But if you reward their barking, you'll never be rid of it. Wait for one of the quiet pauses to interact with the dog, and give her something else to do when you can't be paying attention. Toys that can dispense food (Kongs and Buster Cubes are two good examples) work well, as do treasure hunts (see Chapter 11, Solutions to Common Problems).

Some dogs bark in greeting. Because this is a quiet, short bark or two, meant for the nearby person, and self-limiting, it's rarely a problem for anyone. Other short barks can require a definite response. A louder, very short, very sharp bark conveys annoyance and a warning to end the offending behavior. The dog may have been awakened abruptly, had a foot or tail stepped on or hair pulled. Bitches use the same bark with puppies who are being annoyingly boisterous.

Yet another single bark, this one neither high nor low, with less sharpness than the others, is a definite effort to communicate with humans. It's a canine request for some action, such as opening the door to the backyard or filling the water bowl. People often describe it as "phony," sort of like a faked sneeze. Perhaps, in trying to communicate with us, the dog is trying to sound more human and ends up sounding less canine.

A single, low bark of short duration but high intensity, frequently following a growl, is a warning to back off. This is a confident dog, telling you that you've entered her space, she doesn't like it and you'd better think about leaving—right now. This is not an empty threat. If your dog issues this challenge to anyone other than an intruder, you need to find a good behaviorist and work on some leadership issues before your bark problem becomes a bite problem.

There are also at least a couple of play barks, and they actually do sound more fun-filled than other barks. They generally have a change in pitch or sound within a single bark, so that the bark comes out as two syllables or as a glissando up the scale that almost sounds like a question due to the rising inflection. A dog may bark like this as an invitation to play (with the appropriate body language) or during the excitement of play. This bark combined with a play bow brings up the point that at least some barking may be intended simply to draw attention to the dog's more primary mode of communication, body language—a sort of "look at what I'm telling you" signal.

A device developed in Japan is making its way to American markets. The Bowlingual came from a veterinarian and the Japanese Acoustic Laboratory and is produced by toymaker Takara Co. A small microphone worn on the dog's collar transmits barks to a handheld "translator," which purportedly analyzes the sound and produces an English translation. Claiming to use 200 emotion patterns based on

 You Can Quote Me

I have seen dogs and foxes and coyotes in the Southwest all recognize each others' vocalizations.

Karen Overall, animal behavior specialist

A play bow may be accompanied by barks.

a database of voiceprints and voice analysis, the Bowlingual classes a bark as happy, sad, frustrated, angry, assertive or desiring something. The actual translations say such things as "How dare you," "We're having fun now," "Don't touch me," "I want to play" and so forth.

While this may be an amusing device for dog owners to play around with, relying on its translations to decide on a course of action with a dog seems hazardous. The translations matched up only sporadically with the attitude of the dogs I tested it on, and were sometimes wildly off base. The one capability that may have some application is its data analysis mode, which can track your dog's barking while you are away. For anyone who is suffering a barking problem, or has a dog with separation anxiety, this device could let you know how soon the barking starts, how long it continues and so on.

The device costs the equivalent of $103 in Japan, so it's not just a cute gadget to run out and buy on a whim. But if you're dying to see how it translates *your* dog's barks, it may be a worthwhile purchase.

GROWLS

People generally think of growls as threats. While that may often be correct, other meanings do exist, and some dogs "growl-talk" regularly. Again, it's important to read the whole dog, not just the vocalization. Growls can convey threats, but they also may speak of fear, frustration, insecurity or nothing more noteworthy than the weather.

If a growl is deep, coming from the chest and vibrating up through the dog, beware. If accompanied by stiff body language and raised lips and wrinkled nose, the dog is telling you in no uncertain terms to back off. This growl may end in a short sharp bark, as described previously. If you don't back away and the growling stops, do not assume you've convinced the dog to like you. Unless the body language changes, the dog has determined that her threat (the growl) is not working and there is no choice but to resort to physical violence. When dogs actually attack, they are nearly always silent. People who say a dog "attacked without warning" have usually ignored the vocal threat, misread the body language and pushed the dog to a point where she felt there was no option other than aggression. Some

Think About It

Dog owners often make a serious mistake related to growling. A friend, a veterinarian or a trainer tells them they can't let the dog "get away" with growling. So they start punishing the dog when she growls. And they often do convince the dog not to growl—which means they have extinguished the verbal warning. Now, unless people can read body language appropriately, the dog may bite "without warning."

dogs are punished for growling, in an ill-advised attempt to solve the problem, resulting in a dog who gives no vocal warning of an imminent attack. Most bites could have been avoided if the people had paid more attention to what the dog was saying.

Leaving the area slowly (quick movements are likely to trigger an attack) is certainly advisable. While leaving (or if, for some reason, leaving is not an option), you can use canine calming signals to try to defuse the situation. Turn your side to the dog, avoid direct eye contact (use your peripheral vision), let your chin drop to your chest, blink and yawn. All of these things indicate that you recognize the challenge and you have no wish to fight. If the dog starts blinking back, your message is getting through.

Higher-pitched growls that don't seem to vibrate the dog the way the low-pitched threat growl does, accompanied by a lowered body, lifted lips and wrinkled nose, are the warnings of a less secure dog frightened by the circumstances, but still ready to defend herself should the need arise. This sound, emanating more from the mouth than the chest, equates to what most people think of as a snarl.

As the pitch rises even higher, the growl signifies an even more fearful dog. Dogs whose growls rise and fall through the scale, breaking off and starting again with an occasional high sharp bark thrown in, are terrified. They are literally in fear for their lives, and there's no telling what dogs in this mental state may do. Given the opportunity, they may flee at warp speed, but they could just as easily launch into an all-out attack, what they perceive as a fight to the death.

In general, the higher the pitch of a growl, or the more frequently the pitch varies, the less secure the dog is. This does not mean the dog isn't a threat. All growls intended as a warning should be taken seriously.

One type of growl, however, is meant all in fun. The play growl can be quite noisy and may be low or medium in pitch, but all the body language affirms its playful intent: no teeth are showing, the dog is engaged in friendly chase behaviors or tug games and the growl itself sounds somehow qualitatively different. If you pay attention to your own natural responses to canine communication, without your thought processes getting in the way, you may find that if you hear a serious aggressive threat growl, your stomach tightens and the hair prickles on the back of your neck, while a good play growl makes you smile.

HOWLS

Not all dogs howl. Many of the Nordic breeds, however, "howl-talk" rather than growl-talk. Owners of Alaskan Malamutes and Siberian Huskies are probably familiar with the "woo-woo" their dogs deliver in greeting or to comment on the goings-on. This short happy howl is unique to these dogs and quite unlike the sustained howls used more generally among canines for communication.

The typical wolf howl starts as a howl, often descending from the initial note to a lower drawn-out note. In a wild pack, the howl is joined by others as the pack assembles to hunt, or in a group sing to remind all within earshot that this territory is occupied by a top-notch predator. This is the howl you may hear a dog give in response to a siren or sometimes music. The theory that the sound hurts the dog's ears has been pretty well disproved. It is more likely an atavistic trait, with the dog feeling some instinctive need to answer the sound.

The way humans often attempt to imitate a dog howl ("yip-yip-yip-arooooo") more closely resembles a coyote howl. Coyotes usually operate alone, and may howl to check how close they might be to another's hunting area or simply to hear another voice. In the past, coyotes lived more of a communal life, but in adapting to living in proximity to humans, they became more solitary. So their howls may be cries of loneliness. A dog locked away from his family gives the same sort of howl, and humans recognize a quality of anguished sadness in the sound.

A much more joyful variation of the howl is baying. Many hounds bay when they are on the trail. The sound helps humans, who often can't keep up with their dogs, locate both dog and prey. Baying has more melody than simple howling, with a held sound sliding through many notes. Owners often can recognize the bays of individual dogs and consider some dogs to be more musical than others. Not all dogs in a pack will necessarily bay at once. The ones actually on the scent are the ones who bay, so that others can follow along until they, too, hit the trail.

Howls can sound quite eerie, and plenty of legends have sprung
up around them. Dogs a continent away are said to have howled at
what the family later learned was the moment of the master's death.
(How would anyone remember such a thing so exactly, when it had
no importance at the time, I wonder.) Or the family dog howled
under the master's window as the final moment arrived. (Well, the
dog was probably shut out of the house while the family tended to
the person, and was just declaring his loneliness. He probably howled
more than once, but the one that happened to coincide was the one
remembered.) Howling is actually an awe-inspiring sound without all
the supernatural overtones. In fact, wolf parks offer regular "howl-
ins" where human visitors can howl along with the wolves.

WHINES AND WHIMPERS

Whines and whimpers are sounds of distress or, occasionally, excitement. Their origins lie in puppyhood, when puppies whine if they are
separated from mom or littermates, or when they are cold, hungry or
in distress of any kind. When an adult dog whines, the sound signifies a threat that the dog doesn't want to face but can't avoid (such as
a veterinary exam table) or a desire that the dog can't resolve (needing to go out but facing a closed door). The dog is in psychological
and perhaps also physical distress and is declaring that she is in need
of help.

This distress vocalization is perhaps best described as whimpering. Starting out soft, it quavers at a somewhat high pitch and is
repeated in short bursts. If the dog remains in the distressing situation, the whimpering may grow progressively louder. This sound is an
admission of helplessness, a plea not to be hurt or to be rescued from
the circumstances. A very effective communication indeed, the whim-
per inspires many owners to fuss over their dogs in the vet's office,
patting them nervously, cooing at them and generally confirming the
dog's impression that there is indeed something to be worried about.
It's better to give the dog something else to think about (practicing
some basic words the dog knows, maybe, with a pat and treat for
reward) or to go for a walk around the parking lot until you're called
in to see the veterinarian.

Diamond was whining at this part of the American Temperament Test, hoping to be rescued from the dreaded umbrella.

Nestle makes what we now call his "Timmy's down the well" whine, harking back to the *Lassie* television show. It means he has identified something wrong in his environment and requests our help in dealing with it. We've learned to investigate because he'll persist until the problem is resolved, and it may well be something that really requires our attention. Nestle has told us that Diamond was accidentally locked out of the house, that the chickens had flown into the dog yard, that a sheep was lying upside down in a ditch, plus a number of things we didn't really need to know (the chipmunk is under the deck again!). But he will not be denied in what he deems matters of importance.

A louder whine, less heart-rending but more persistent, comes from a dog who has learned it's an effective way to get attention. The dog will often look at the owner, whine, then look at some desired object such as food or a toy. The request makes itself quite clear. The sound doesn't rise and fall in the same way as the distress whine, and the dog often fidgets and dances with impatience to get her way.

A dog suddenly interested in something in the environment may whine, but the sound is much lower in pitch and usually consists of one or two drawn-out sounds.

Finally, a string of short, truncated whines with a slightly breathless sound is a sign of excitement or an invitation to play. The dog can barely contain her eagerness, and it leaks out in this vocalization. Though still a whine, it sounds quite different from the cries of distress.

OTHER VOCALIZATIONS

Dogs commonly make another half-dozen or so sounds (plus those sounds that are particular to an individual). Most of these sounds are fairly limited in their use and meanings.

Yelps can come singly or in groups. A single yelp is usually a quick, short and very high-pitched sound in reaction to sudden pain. It's very similar to us yelling "ow!" when we stub a toe. A series of yelps, on the other hand, often expressed as "kai yai," indicates a high level of fear and/or hurt. A dog fleeing a fight after a beating will often yelp as she goes.

The sounds that dogs make in anticipation of a pleasurable experience are often hard to describe. Nestle makes a sound like a play growl crossed with a whine, and the closest I can come to writing it down phonetically is "owr owr owr ruff wow." It's in the mid-low range, and it's accompanied by a lot of movement. Other dogs may use more of a toned-down howl, something like "woooo-hoooo-wah."

Dogs sigh in almost precisely the same way as humans. First there's the lovely sigh of contentment. A dog who's had a good outing and has now come back to settle by the fire with her owner may lie down, put her chin on her paws, narrow or close her eyes and sigh. It's akin to a human eating a big dinner, pushing back from the table, settling down into the chair and sighing with pleasure.

Think About It

So, if dogs laugh, do they have a sense of humor? Though evidence is anecdotal, many would say yes. I know that Serling did. He devised many unique ways to break up the boredom of obedience competition, and he invariably smiled when he pulled them on me. He positively beamed when spectators laughed.

You can almost hear the sigh this dog gave when he was asked to pose for a picture.

For both dogs and humans, sighing can also mean disappointment. If the dog has been trying to elicit some behavior from her human—playing fetch or getting a treat—and the desired response hasn't been forthcoming, the dog may give up, lie down, put her muzzle on her paws and with eyes wide open, sigh. It's a sign of surrender and giving up the effort.

Some dogs will grunt as a greeting or to solicit attention, or even as an alternate sound of contentment. A mechanical sound is tooth snapping, where the dog forcefully brings the jaws together to make a sharp sound. Some dogs use it in play, while others use it as a back-off signal when things get a little too frenetic. Another somewhat mechanical sound is panting. The dog may be excited or tense, and the breathing comes fast, open-mouthed and audible. Other occasional sounds include groaning (in distress or sometimes contentment), puffing (with the lips blowing out at the sides, used to signal submission) and though rarely heard, hissing (always a sound of submission).

A researcher at Sierra Nevada College, Patricia Simonet, identified a sound like a pant, but more breathy. She found it occurred only during play and labeled it a dog laugh. The closest I can come in

Although Serling was quite a talented dog, no one could ever quite figure out the message when he answered the phone.

Did a deer pass this way? Did someone drop a morsel of cinnamon roll? The dogs know.

writing it down is "henh henh henh." Simonet did spectrographic analysis on recordings of the "laugh" and found it significantly different from a regular pant. Dogs also responded to recordings of the laugh by soliciting play.

Many dogs have sounds unique to themselves. You might know a sound only your dog does, and you probably find it endearing. I know I miss Serling's hum very, very much.

Finally, there is a third language that dogs use, based on scent. You may find it annoying when you're trying to jog and your dog is trying to stop and sniff every rose along the way, but if we could gain as much information from scent as the dog can, we'd be down there sniffing too. Scent is the reason behind the canine greeting ritual of sniffing each other, and scent plays a large role in the canine environment. We're just not endowed to understand this part of their language.

CHAPTER 7

Best of Breed

How did we get so many breeds; what are they meant for?
Do you need to communicate with or train different breeds in different ways?

> A dog is not "almost human" and I know of no greater insult
> to the canine race than to describe it as such. The dog can do
> many things which man cannot do, never could do, and never
> will do.
>
> John Holmes

*Shauna and her friend Kerry stood ringside watching the action in the Open
obedience ring. Dogs soared over jumps and retrieved dumbbells, stayed at their
owners' side without a leash, and not only came when called but dropped into a
down position right in the middle of coming. "I'm going to do that with Barney
some day," Shauna said. She was shocked when Kerry laughed. "Don't be ridiculous. Barney's a Beagle. Everyone knows Beagles are cute, but stubborn and not
so bright." Shauna turned away so Kerry wouldn't see how hurt she was.
Barney wasn't dumb! She knew he wasn't dumb. But a nagging little voice told
her that Kerry had a lot more experience than she did. Kerry, unaware of the
effect her words were having, continued. "I'd compete with MacGregor—
he's really bright. But of course you can't have Scottish terriers around all
these others dogs."*

Could this be true? Are Beagles stupid and Scottish Terriers aggressive? Can all our problems with our dogs be traced to breed characteristics? Of course they can't. In fact, many of the behaviors classed as
problems—barking, digging, chasing—are normal canine behaviors,
expressed more strongly in certain breeds and particular individuals

Stupid? Me? I don't think so!

than in others. Many of the comments you may hear about one breed or another are simply false, totally outdated or have a kernel of truth embedded in an exaggerated statement. We'll take a look at groups, breeds, mixed breeds and even animals other than dogs in this chapter, and get it all sorted out.

STEREOTYPES AND IDIOSYNCRASIES

The Groups

The stereotypes actually start with the Groups, a device used by dog registries such as the American Kennel Club to compartmentalize

You Can Quote Me

Dogs are much more adaptable than we are. . . . Don't get fixated on "breed behaviors," because that confuses things. If a behavior increases in frequency or intensity, it is being reinforced, whether you're doing the reinforcement or not.

Kerry Haynes-Lovell

breeds into supposedly logical sets. In reality, these are not all that logical and vary from registry to registry. The AKC sorts dogs into the following groups:

Sporting

Working

Herding

Hounds

Terriers

Toys

Non-Sporting

Back in the 1880s, there were only two classifications: Sporting (hunting) dogs and Non-Sporting (all the other breeds). The Hound Group was broken out of the Sporting Group. Other groups gradually emerged from the Non-Sporting Group, leaving odds and ends behind. Unfortunately, some breeds got lumped into groups that don't really suit them. The Norwegian Elkhound, for example, is in the Hound Group even though it obviously has much more in common with Siberian Huskies (Working Group) or Keeshonden (the plural of Keeshond, who remain in the Non-Sporting Group) than with either Basset Hounds or Salukis. Some Poodle people have been advocating moving their breed from Non-Sporting to Sporting, to reflect the breed's hunting background.

The United Kennel Club recognizes eight groups, only a few of which correspond to the AKC breakdown. They are

Gun Dogs

Scenthounds

Herding

Guarding Dogs

Sighthounds

Terriers

Companion Dogs

Northern Breeds

I like the idea of breaking the hounds into Scenthounds and Sighthounds. Personality-wise, it's much more logical. Collecting the Northern Breeds—those with the fox faces and curled tails—into one place, regardless of size, also makes good sense. Basing a group not on size (Toy Group) but on function (Companion Dogs) also seems a step in the right direction.

The international registry, the FCI (Federation Cynologique Internationale) breaks things down even further, using 10 groups:

Sheepdogs and Cattledogs

Pinschers and Schnauzers, Swiss Mountain Dogs and
   Swiss Cattledogs

Terriers

Dachshunds

Spitz and Primitive Types

Scenthounds

Pointing Dogs

Retrievers, Flushing Dogs, Water Dogs

Companion and Toy Dogs

Sighthounds

Dachshunds are earthdogs every bit as much as the terriers.

Giving Dachshunds their own category, and breaking hunting dogs into two separate groups (Pointing Dogs and Retrievers, etc.), does seem a bit much. The UKC's eight groups provide the most functional breakdown, but still, making sweeping generalizations across the individual breeds in a group is risky business.

One dog food company offers separate foods formulated for each of the AKC's groups. However, a single food that is supposedly targeted to both a Greyhound and a Bloodhound doesn't seem to make much sense.

Still, you do hear people make generalizations about the groups. Some say terriers don't get along with others dogs and herding dogs nip people. Delve into these stereotypes and you'll find that in dog shows, terrier handlers often hold their dogs on tight leashes, facing each other in close proximity. The dogs are expected to "show terrier attitude," to posture and rear up and maybe even bark or growl. These dogs may learn that this behavior gets approval from their humans, and adopt it outside the ring. Left to their own devices, some terriers are perfectly happy to be friends with other dogs. They are generally a feisty bunch—they had to be to go down burrows after rats and badgers—but much of how they respond to other dogs depends on how they are taught to behave as puppies.

Herding dogs were bred to herd. So it should come as no surprise that they're generally happier when their family is all together in one place—and nipping is one way they accomplish this. Even within the Herding Group, though, some dogs nip and some don't. Those that do can be taught that such behavior is inappropriate with people.

So knowing the group to which your dog belongs (breeds are listed by group at both the AKC and UKC Web sites, which you can find in the Resources section at the back of the book) can give you a vague idea of a dog's characteristics, but not much more.

The Breeds

To illustrate some of the problems associated with assigning characteristics to breeds, I asked participants in a dog book discussion e-mail list to send me stereotypical remarks that they had heard made about breeds. Some of what they described as the "worst" stereotypes were:

- Akitas are Japanese fighting dogs and natural killers.
- English Springer Spaniels are hyper.
- Afghan Hounds are stupid.
- Australian Shepherds bite.
- Border Collies are crazy.
- Yorkshire Terriers are "froo froo" dogs who are not good for anything.
- Norwegian Elkhounds bark a lot.
- Golden Retrievers and Labrador Retrievers are gentle and would never bite anyone.
- Jack Russell Terriers are wired.

 You Can Quote Me

When owners have preconceptions about a breed's ability, dogs lose out and fail to reach their potential, which can only be achieved by training and socialization. We do not share a dog's senses or its way of understanding the world. Nonetheless, many of us are tempted to try to define a dog's intelligence by comparing it to that of other animals, to that of humans, and by comparing one breed with another. This is a waste of time. A dog is not dumb because it cannot do algebra. Better to look at the way a dog responds to and manipulates its environment (or its owner).

Ian Dunbar, *Dog Behavior*

- German Shepherds are fear biters.
- Pit Bulls are aggressive, untrustworthy, maul babies and kill other dogs. (Several people took pains to point out that Pit Bulls actually have some of the most stable temperaments of all dogs.)

Some of the stereotypes that the discussion participants deemed a bit more accurate were:

- Norwegian Elkhounds shed a lot. (The breeder reporting this affirms that with the correct coat for the breed, shedding is inevitable.)
- Lhasa Apsos develop many strange behaviors, and the darker colors tend to have aggression problems (from a behaviorist).
- Border Collies and Australian Shepherds are supersensitive, especially regarding sound, and require more socialization than other dogs.
- Boxers have a very upright body posture that other dogs may misread.
- Rottweilers, Doberman Pinschers and Pit Bulls may be unsuitable for first-time dog owners (perhaps due as much to public perception as to behavior).

 ## Think About It

If you are old enough, think back 20 or 30 years. What dog was in the news then as the "dangerous" breed? (Hint: It wasn't a Pit Bull.) Why would one breed suddenly stop being "dangerous" and another breed start? Do you know what breed consistently ranks at or near the top of the incidence of dog bites list? Cocker Spaniels. The people they bite are nearly always family members. But no one goes around proclaiming them to be dangerous dogs and suggesting that they be banned from existence. Why do you think that is? (Hint: Consider a Cocker Spaniel's looks compared to that of a Pit Bull or a Rottweiler. Looks can be deceiving.)

People fling these kinds of statements around all the time. And without being familiar with many of the breeds mentioned, determining whether there's any truth to them is nearly impossible. It's best to take any such statements with a healthy grain of salt. Kathy Sdao notes that in her extensive experience, individual differences are greater than breed differences. There may often be more variation of behavior between two dogs of the same breed than between two individuals of different breeds.

German Shepherd Dogs have long been a well-respected breed, and were often depicted on utilitarian items.

Still, there are some breed peculiarities of note. For example, Chow Chows do have quite a different structure of their hindquarters, giving them a stilted gait that is unlike other dogs. Other dogs seem to misread this stance— Chows are not known for great dog sociability. Your best bet is to discuss breed characteristics with a reputable breeder, who can tell you the potential bad along with the good.

Addressing the AKC's assertion that "with a purebred dog, you know what you're getting," Karen Overall was blunt. "You're getting a dog that somebody paid $9 to register." She did agree that with a specific breed you can get a general idea of what the dog will look like when she grows up, a general idea of size when full-grown (not a trivial consideration, in many cases) and some idea of the basic behaviors selected for in making breeding decisions. But that's far from the depth of knowledge implied by "you know what you're getting."

Overall also pointed out that general breed characteristics can change over the years. Baby boomers and their elders remember Doberman Pinschers as the killer dogs in Nazi concentration camps, then in the news back home as hypersensitive, aggressive biters. As a

You Can Quote Me

If people can understand that retrievers are prone to pick things up and carry them, terriers like to dig and bark at movement, Beagles to 'run away' from their owners making lots of noise, it becomes easier to tolerate and work with those idiosyncrasies. I've seen basic examples of breed patterns repeated over and over again, but a clever owner can always work around them if they are willing to put in the time. You have to work harder to get a terrier to retrieve than a Golden, but it *can* still be done.

Mandy Book, author and dog trainer

result, breeders made it their business to concentrate on temperament and, if anything, went too far in the other direction. Dobermans today are generally sweet, perhaps even overly fearful dogs. While breeds may change, public sentiment doesn't always change with them.

A survey conducted by behaviorist Bonnie Beaver (and discussed in *Canine Behavior: A Guide for Veterinarians*) revealed that breed considerations hardly factor into how people choose a dog. When she asked her clients why they had chosen a specific dog:

- 24 percent chose based on sex
- 17 percent chose a "friendly/affectionate" dog
- 15 percent chose out of pity for a particular dog
- 14 percent chose a "cute" dog
- 12 percent chose based on color
- 12 percent chose based on size
- 14 percent chose based on general appearance or other physical characteristics

So perhaps breed characteristics aren't as important as the AKC would like to think, at least among the population at large. Otherwise, how would you explain the popularity of our next subject—mixed breeds?

Mixed Breeds

Dogs of mixed or uncertain origin are actually the most popular "breed" in the United States. I happen to be an aficionado of mixes and particularly shelter rescues. I enjoy starting without the preconceived notions that come along with purebreds and learning the dog's characteristics by getting to know her as an individual. Yet, even with mixed breeds, you'll hear some sweeping generalizations, such as:

- Mixes are smarter than purebreds.
- Mixes have "hybrid vigor" and are healthier than purebreds.
- You never know what you're going to get with a mix.
- You can't enter dog sports with a mix.
- Shelter dogs are in a shelter because they're behavioral misfits.

Let's take these statements one at a time, starting at the bottom and working up. Young puppies can hardly have been surrendered because of behavior problems, unless you consider such normal puppy behaviors as peeing, pooping and crying at night to be "problems." Puppies end up at shelters for a variety of reasons that aren't their doing. Too many people with unneutered dogs simply have puppies they don't want. Then there are parents who want their children to "witness the miracle of birth" but then don't want the fuss and bother of raising puppies. Puppies end up at shelters when people who thought that puppy breeding would be a quick and easy way to make some extra money find out that no one wants to pay for their "product." However it happened, the puppies arrived, weren't wanted and were hauled off to the shelter. You can hardly pin behavior problems on the poor things.

Older dogs could be equally blameless (look in the classified ads of your paper and see how many "moving—can't take dog" ads you find there) or could indeed have some behavioral bugs that need to be worked out. Believe it or not, some people want perpetual puppies, and surrender one dog after another once the pet reaches adolescence. Others refuse to make any effort toward training the dog and blame any consequences on her. Unless the shelter staff has marked the dog as potentially aggressive or a confirmed biter, don't assume that the dog has arrived at the shelter due to bad behavior.

Much of the behavior you see in dogs in shelters is highly uncharacteristic of the dogs' personalities. The confinement, close proximity to other dogs and sporadic interaction with people create a high level of stress. Some dogs react by barking and jumping wildly whenever people come into view. Some become depressed and show no interest in anything happening around them. This is not their true character.

Many shelters today do a much better job of walking dogs and playing with them on a regular basis, even noting on their pens how well they walk on leash, how they do when greeting other dogs and other pertinent information. Most have a room or a yard where you can be alone with your prospect to try to get a truer idea of personality. Keep in mind that plenty of people have chosen what they thought was a very quiet reserved individual, only to find themselves with a doggie dynamo once they settled in at home. The more interaction

Nestle (right), part Australian Kelpie and large part mystery (though Ibizan Hound is a possibility) and Diamond (left), listed by the shelter as a Maltese mix.

Try It Yourself

When you're out and about, keep your eyes open for mixed breeds. Whenever you see one, try to figure out what breeds might have combined to create that look and personality. Keep in mind that there may be more than two breeds involved and that some breeds tend to have a stronger influence. Black Labs usually create black, smooth-coated, retriever-type dogs. German Shepherds tend to impart longer backs to any of their offspring as well as characteristic shepherd coat markings. If you have the opportunity, ask the dog's owner if he or she knows any of the breeds in the dog's makeup, so you can see how you did.

you can have away from the shelter, the more likely you'll see at least a glimmer of the dog's true self.

Don't take the breed descriptions you may find on the pens too seriously unless the shelter can assure you that they have some really experienced multibreed experts on staff or helping out. At a lot of shelters, you'll find nearly every dog identified as a German Shepherd Dog cross, Labrador Retriever cross, Beagle cross, Poodle cross or Pit Bull. Although some of these labels may be accurate, odds are a lot won't be.

If you have any experienced dog friends, take one with you to the shelter. He or she can help you decipher the mixes of breeds and assist in determining personality.

Returning to our list of misconceptions about mixed breeds, one says you can't compete in canine sports with a mixed breed. Matches and trials may not be as abundant as they are for purebreds, but they do exist. Years ago, the United Kennel Club began registering spayed or neutered mixed breeds and welcoming them to compete in obedience and agility. They've now added weight pulls, and other sports are in the works. UKC calls mixed breeds AMBOR dogs because the American Mixed Breed Obedience Registry (AMBOR) worked with the UKC to put the program together. My dog Serling was one of the first mixes to be registered with the UKC. AMBOR still exists, helping mixed breeds achieve titles in other areas, such as tracking. The United States Dog Agility Association (USDAA) has never cared about the background of dogs entering their trials, and the American Herding Breeds Association (AHBA) permits mixes of herding breeds in their events. Clever Canine Companions awards all dogs for all sorts of achievements, such as pet therapy and hiking, and Wet Dogs does the same in water tests. Mixed Breed Dog Clubs of America even offers conformation (a traditional dog show), though their clubs are active only in scattered pockets of the country. If you have a mix and you want to compete, the opportunities are there.

As for the idea that mixes are smarter than purebreds, don't believe it. There are brilliant mixes and dumb-as-a-rock purebreds, but the opposite is also true. Intelligence is an individual trait—one we aren't very good at assessing in other humans, let alone in other species (more about this in a moment).

The concept of "hybrid vigor" does at least have a little science behind it. There's a reason for the societal taboo on marrying your brother, after all. Mixing the genes from a more varied gene pool reduces the chance of offspring suffering detrimental or even lethal gene combinations that cause epilepsy, cancer, hip dysplasia and most of the other serious disorders known in dogs. Some conditions are now so prevalent across breeds that the odds don't improve very much even in mixes. So while there's a smidgeon of truth to the idea of hybrid vigor, choosing a mixed breed is no guarantee that you are choosing a dog free of genetic imperfections.

Finally let's address the idea that you never know what you're going to get with a mix. Personally, I like the uncertainty. I think it helps you pay more attention to the dog's individual eccentricities. If size as an adult is important, however, those with canine experience can make reasonably accurate predictions. Look for a dog you are attracted to, whose activity level suits your lifestyle. Don't ignore purebred rescue groups even if you want a mix—many of them also will keep an eye out for crosses that are identifiably part their breed of choice.

COMMUNICATION GAMES SUITED TO BREEDS

Nearly all the trainers I know switched to positive means of training long ago, using either lure and reward methods or clicker training. Although there are plenty of choke collar trainers still out there, my own experiences and those of others convince me that positive methods are the tools of choice. If they fail you for some reason, you can always proceed to more forceful methods. You haven't lost anything.

Clicker trainer Morgan Spector uses the ancient oath to "do no harm" as his prime training directive. Of course, you have to be able to read your dog and understand the response your training is creating to *know* if you are doing any harm. Remember, communication is a two-way street. You need to do your best not only to make your language clear to the dog, but also to realize what the dog is telling you. The dog will tell you what you are doing right or wrong. If your dog starts throwing calming signals at you or starts to show evident stress in your presence, you are doing something wrong. Fixing it may mean taking your dog out of a highly charged situation, quitting for the day or completely changing your training routine.

Many trainers I have spoken with lean heavily toward clicker training (a specific form of what is scientifically called operant conditioning). Morgan Spector notes he has found that soft-tempered rescue doges respond well because clicker training is not a stressful method, while hard-headed terriers respond equally well because it challenges their intelligence and tenacity. Kathy Sdao began her career

 You Can Quote Me

Because different breeds of dogs have differing sensitivities to motivation and learning, the application of any training technique will invariably have to account for those differences. Adapting a training strategy to a particular breed type is not the end of the adaptation, however. Any given population of dogs includes overly sensitive and incredibly insensitive dogs who respond differently to aversive training methods—the former go belly up and the latter appear to thrive. The opposite reaction occurs with dogs who are highly sensitive to positive reinforcement and others who are indifferent to food and affection—either because of early neglect or breed type. Though breed types can give us a starting place for training, it is by no means an automatic or all-inclusive consideration. Ultimately, we must always strive to go farther and create a form of communication that embraces each dog as an individual.

Gary Wilkes, columnist and founder of Click & Treat

using operant conditioning on dolphins, whales and walruses, and saw no reason to switch her training methodology when she started training dogs. She quotes Karen Pryor, an early proponent of clicker training, as saying that the technique works with "any species that eats and has a brain stem." Sdao says, "If it can be used successfully to train birds, fish, cats, llamas and elephants, it certainly can work with Poodles *and* Pit Bulls." Mandy Book believes clicker training is a method anyone can use. It prevents the relationship between dog and owner from becoming adversarial, and it requires owners to have a better understanding of their dogs. Meanwhile, dogs love it.

Still, there are some potential problems to take into account when considering clicker training. Sound-sensitive dogs (remember my earlier comment about Border Collies and Australian Shepherds) may actually find the two-tone sound of the clicker aversive. In this case, you can simply use a verbal marker instead ("Yes"), or a retractable pen—much quieter than a clicker. With deaf dogs, you can flick a flashlight on and off instead of clicking a clicker, or use a special vibrating collar (*not* a shock collar—this one just vibrates, like a pager or cell phone).

Most people use food as the reward associated with the clicker, and this raises two further considerations. First, where you deliver the treat is important. If you want the dog to heel on your left, but you give the treat in front of you, you'll find yourself tripping over the dog, who wants to get to where the treat will be. Use the dog's position to your advantage and give the treat when the dog is where you want her to be. If you have a small dog, you may have to work on limbering

---

 You Can Quote Me

Dogs are neither stupid nor quasi-human. Evolution has ensured that they are exactly as smart as they need to be in order to survive and thrive. People who tell me their dog is stupid typically have trained them, albeit inadvertently, to be stubborn and unresponsive. The responsibility often lies with the trainer, not the dog's genetic heritage.
Kathy Sdao, animal trainer and behavior specialist

up! Second, and more serious, too many treats can have health consequences. Too much high-fat food can create pancreatitis, a serious medical condition, particularly seen in toy breeds. You certainly don't want to make your dog obese, either. Take a portion of your dog's daily kibble, mix it with some goodies such as hot dog slices or small lumps of cheese, and use it for your training sessions.

Also remember that food is not the only reward. Though it's easy to use and works well with the majority of dogs, there are other options. Many dogs will work enthusiastically for the chance to play with a favorite toy. We'll talk more about games to play with your dog in a moment.

INTELLIGENCE AND THE NATURE/NURTURE CONTROVERSY

Books purporting to examine the intelligence of dogs have largely done a disservice to canines. Ranking one breed against another on the basis of obedience trials is hardly a key to true intelligence. Dogs who do well in training situations are certainly biddable—willing to figure out and repeatedly do what their handler wants—but not necessarily intelligent. In fact, Ian Dunbar comments, "Dogs might argue that easily trainable dogs are pretty dumb and that a smart dog trains its owner!"

Some breeds were historically adapted to operate on their own rather than to obey commands from a master. Earthdogs didn't pop out of tunnels when humans called—they were dragged out, often by their characteristically sturdy little tails. Sighthounds were expected to see the prey and give chase. It was up to the humans to keep up, often on horseback—and Arabian horses were developed for this purpose along with sighthounds.

Researchers now hypothesize that dogs have three types of intelligence:

- Instinctive intelligence (behavioral tendencies, genetically determined abilities)
- Obedience or working intelligence
- Adaptive intelligence

*Tibetan Terriers are terriers in name only. Expecting them
to behave the same as other dogs in the Terrier Group
will lead you astray.*

Instinctive intelligence may make a dog a genius in one area
(sheep herding, for example) while rendering her handicapped in
another (a herding dog may find it difficult to lie still while children
run around and play). So which level of "intelligence" should you
assess?

According to Dunbar, it's adaptive intelligence that we should be
examining, focusing on learning through problem solving, observation and insight. Can a dog learn through observation, by watching
another dog do something? Handlers involved in field trials and herding regularly teach young dogs by working them with experienced
dogs. Some researchers are setting up refined studies to assess this
ability in dogs. You may see adaptive intelligence in action if you have
multiple dogs in your household. If you've taught one dog to sit up
and beg and she gets attention and treats for this, you just might see
the other dog working to develop the same behavior. Diamond is
asked to "sing" before going out the front door for the daily outing.
Nestle had never been taught to speak. But when Diamond was slow
to vocalize, Nestle jumped in with his own version of singing.

Problem solving and insight often get dogs into trouble. In *Canine
Behavior: A Guide for Veterinarians*, Bonnie Beaver tells the story of a dog
who escaped the yard by climbing on a pile of wood. Her people
moved the pile away from the fence, thinking they had solved the

problem. But the dog did some problem solving of his own by moving the wood back, one piece at a time, climbing on the pile he made and escaping again. These are the kinds of dogs who require resourceful owners with highly developed senses of humor and willingness to work at staying one step ahead of their dogs.

But where does intelligence come from? Does it relate to inborn abilities (nature) or the environment in which the animal is raised (nurture)? The answer, as Karen Overall says, is yes, meaning that it's nature *and* nurture, inextricably intertwined. "Genetics gives you the foundation on which environmental responses can be built. Each individual is endowed with a certain amount of adaptability. Their environment then determines how well that adaptability is maximized." Your dog can't be more than her genetic makeup allows, but you can have a tremendously positive impact by providing a safe but challenging environment throughout your dog's life. That environment includes the games you play with your dog.

GOOD GAMES FOR GREAT DOGS

If you listen to trainers and behaviorists, you will hear considerable disagreement about what games people should or shouldn't play with their dogs. Tug-of-war is the game trainers most strongly warn against. Some say that it makes the dog aggressive and encourages biting. Yet other behaviorists are just as vehemently in favor of tug-of-war. Terry Ryan pinpoints the real reason behind a lot of the disagreement when she says, "Tug-of-war is fine for all dogs, if the owner knows and implements the proper rules when needed. Since not all owners are able to do that. . . ."

Kathy Sdao is vehemently in favor of tug games. "I *insist* that my clients teach their dogs to play tug of war," she says. "It's a great game with a lousy name! The game isn't owner versus dog. It's owner and dog versus the stuffed bunny, the tug toy."

According to Sdao, there are significant benefits to this type of game, including:

- Tug provides deeply satisfying reinforcement for good behavior, especially coming when called.
- Tug gives dogs a way to burn off energy.

- Tug lets dogs vent some predatory instincts in a safe way.
- Tug teaches dogs to control their mouths around human flesh.
- Tug creates a bond between owner and dog.

Research done by Nicola Rooney at the University of Southampton completely negates the idea that playing tug increases aggression. She found no link at all between the game and the problem.

The key is that the game must come with a firm set of rules. Only by following these rules can these benefits be realized and the problems avoided. The rules are

- Humans own the tug toy and keep it in a safe place, inaccessible to the dog.
- Humans start the tug game—the dog is not allowed to shove a toy at a family member to initiate play.
- Humans end the game.
- The dog will give the toy to the owner on cue, immediately, every time.
- The game ends instantly if the dog's teeth ever touch human skin or if the dog refuses to give the toy to the human.
- The human frequently asks the dog to perform brief obedience behaviors such as sit or down during the game, to maintain control and momentarily calm the dog.
- Older children play this game only with active adult supervision, and younger children don't play it at all.
- Growling is OK.

Jean Donaldson, Director of Training at the San Francisco SPCA, agrees that games based on the "predatory sequence"—find, chase, grab, kill, dissect and eat—are valuable outlets for canine energy and instincts. The slippery slope argument against tug games implies that the dog has no desire to behave in this fashion unless prompted by the owner, but, of course, dogs do want to chew and grab and tug. By playing games that involve these activities you can channel the dog's energy (which is there whether you tap into it or not)—into games that you can control. If you don't channel the energy, then the dog is likely to improvise, and you may not appreciate the results. The dominance argument—that if you let the dog win, it will alter the dog's rank with the owner—is equally unfounded. Predation (which is the basis for these games) is entirely separate from rank. Wolves trying to bring down a bison or moose aren't trying to see who gets the leg—they're cooperating to accomplish the kill.

Donaldson echoes Terry Ryan in admitting that there is some potential for problems. "Any rough game in the hands of an idiot can get out of hand, but in the hands of an idiot anything can go bad." She also says that tug, in particular, is a fine way to check the measure of control you have when your dog is excited.

Donaldson recommends four games in addition to tug, relating them to the different stages of predatory behavior. For the finding of food stage, she recommends treasure hunts, or what she calls search and rescue. To teach the dog to play, you hide a toy or a stuffed chew in an easy place and encourage the dog to find it, helping as necessary. When the dog finds it, play a quick game of tug. As the dog catches on to the game, owners should help less and less so that the dog learns to rely on her nose. This can be an interactive game, or you can leave the house mined with hidden treasures while you're out.

For the chase segment of predation, Donaldson recommends retrieving, and notes that *any* dog can be conditioned to retrieve. She calls it the perfect counterconditioning to the common problem of object guarding (which occurs when a dog refuses to let a person take some object from her) because retrieving involves surrendering the object so that the owner can make it "run away" again.

An alternative game for the chase stage is keep-away. Dogs are always trying to get someone to chase them—that's the motivation behind grabbing an object and dancing just out of reach. There are rules with keep-away, just as there are with tug. The owner always initiates the game and only plays with "legal" objects (either one the owner specifically selects or any of the dog's toys). Then the human alternates with either a series of retrieves or games of tug-of-war (both cooperative games). A final, important rule is that games of keep-away must incorporate an "off switch," a cue to stop. For safety, owners should chase their dogs rather than the other way around.

Tug-of-war represents the grabbing and holding section of predatory behavior, and we've already laid down the basic rules for playing it.

Finally, you and your dog can play "dissection," ripping open prey once its killed, by sacrificing stuffed animals. Or, you can tie a treat up in a series of knotted rags and let the dog have at it. To those who argue that this will encourage the dog to tear up everything in the house, Donaldson points out that dogs focus more on particulars and can certainly differentiate a stuffed toy from a couch. In fact, my dogs have their own stuffed toys, which Nestle delights in tearing to pieces, but they do not touch our teddy bears posing in a basket on the floor or the stuffed dogs sitting on a low child's chair. They know what's theirs.

Giving dogs daily doses of predatory behavior that let them get it out of their system can result in fewer behavior problems.

There are a few breed or group considerations to keep in mind, however. First, many of the toy dogs have problems with their teeth, so tugging might not be such a good idea for them. If you are in doubt, ask your veterinarian. Terriers generally love to rip things apart, and also love to dig (see Chapter 11, Solutions to Common Problems, for how to work out a digging compromise). Scenthounds live to use their noses, so working on tracking together (see Chapter 12, Now We're Talking) will suit them. Sighthounds respond to movement, and will probably like chasing a Frisbee or a rag tied to the end of a lunge whip (a horse training device you can find at feed or tack stores). Retrievers, of course, love to retrieve, and there are all sorts of devices to aid in throwing balls for their owners. Herding dogs would love to herd if they could, but if you don't have a flock of sheep handy for your dog, they also like Frisbees or agility training. Working breeds work in different ways. Some were born to pull, and this can be on wheels as well as on snow. Others want to work in partnership with their humans, and competitions such as obedience, freestyle and agility will suit them just fine. Non-sporting dogs don't have much in common with one another, but nearly all of them enjoy a chance to get out and sniff the world and have a good run around. (Chapter 12, Now We're Talking, will look further at things to do with your dog.)

A daily walk can be beneficial for both dogs and humans.

Treasure hunts should only be played with toys if your dog has a weight problem or other medical issues. If you already have behavioral issues, you need to get help and work them out first before playing some of these games. But these games will help in increasing your bond with your dog *and* allow you to keep an eye on your level of control. Dogs need to be stimulated mentally, not only through training of basic commands, but also through games designed to make them think. Dogs need to be exercised every day and require social interaction. Donaldson notes that if zoo animals were kept under the same totally boring conditions as many of our dogs, it would be considered inhumane.

EVEN CHICKENS CAN BE TRAINED

Anyone who's been told, or read, or just gotten it into their heads that their breed or dog is too stupid, stubborn or otherwise incapable of learning should think about this: Experienced dog trainers flock to camps to further hone their skills by training chickens. That's right, chickens. Your dog's smarter than a chicken, isn't she?

A chicken learning to negotiate the weave poles at a chicken training camp.

Actually, chickens make an excellent training prospect. They offer lots of behavior very quickly and they respond well to food rewards. The speed of their actions means that the trainer really has to be on top of his or her game or the reinforcer (the clicker) will be delivered late and won't be marking the desired behavior. Timing becomes much more critical.

Imagine how much easier it is to work with your dog, a creature you not only know well (or should!), but one much more in tune with interspecies social living. So no excuses.

It doesn't matter whether you want to fly to the heights of obedience or agility or simply have a well-behaved pet. Understanding your dog, throwing away all those breed stereotypes and mixing play and training will see you to your goals.

CHAPTER 8

A Touching Experience

Can touch be a form of communication?
Do the benefits of touch flow both ways?

> The evidence favoring the health value of pets is so compelling that if pet therapy were a pill, we would not be able to manufacture it fast enough.
>
> Dr. Larry Dossey

A Klamath legend explains how the dog became domesticated (and may not be far off the mark). Two wolf brothers killed a deer in the mountains. They wanted to cook it but they had no fire. The older wolf told his brother to go down to the Indians camped in the valley and steal fire. Younger brother went to the camp to do as he was told, but there were bones and scraps of meat lying around the tepees and he was very hungry. He began to eat the scraps. The Indians in the tepee saw the young wolf, but were careful not to scare him away. They even threw out more bones. When he was full, younger brother went back to his brother on the mountain. "I could not steal fire," he said. "There were too many people around."

Older brother sent him down again, and again younger brother ate bones and meat and came back without fire. A third trip went the same way, only this time the older wolf was so angry that he told his brother "Bring back fire or do not come back!" So the younger wolf went and stayed in the Indian village. Soon the Indians let him in the tepees, where it was nice and warm. The older wolf came and called to his brother at night, but the Indians fed and petted younger brother and kept him warm. He stayed and became the Indians' dog.

Before we get involved in the wonderful details of what touching your dog can do to benefit both of you, it's important to consider a few things. First, not all dogs appreciate being touched. With some it may simply be a lack of experience, and you can change their minds through practice, but others just don't seem to like having their personal space invaded. Second, not all touch is beneficial, and poking in the wrong places can actually be hazardous. As veterinarian Dennis Wilcox points out, the points used in acupressure and acupuncture are precisely the same points referenced in martial arts. They can be used to heal or to harm. This is why I don't recommend that amateurs try to use acupressure techniques. Sticking to more general massage is safer. Third, while massage can be a wonderful thing for older dogs or those recovering from physical ailments, you do need to be more cautious about what you do and how you do it.

We'll examine all these points further as we go along, but don't let them discourage you. Dogs who are accustomed to being handled make much better companions.

PSYCHOLOGICAL BENEFITS OF TOUCH

In a somewhat startling revelation, a survey of U.S. lifestyles in the year 2000 revealed that more households included pets than children. Dr. Jonica Newby provides an illuminating explanation of this in her book, *The Animal Attraction*: "One of the most basic social contact

---

 You Can Quote Me

Dogs have an extremely high Pettable-Patable index and a Snuggly-Huggable quotient through the roof. The dog's delightful furriness makes it most pleasant to stroke and groom. Moreover, stroking a dog is soothing. It relieves stress, calms the nerves and gets the old alpha rhythms going on in the brain. And dogs seem to lap up the affection and give it back in trumps. Dogs make you feel wanted. Basically, the dog body is a conveniently sized feel-good companion/ psychologist combo.

Ian Dunbar, *Dog Behavior*

Pet therapy visits bring dogs into the often sterile environment of care facilities, and offer patients a chance to cuddle a furry body.

qualities of all is touch. Without touch, infants fail to develop normally. But our culture has almost severed our capacity for touch. Except with our pets. Cats and dogs are both superbly tactile. So here's the problem. We *must* achieve zero population growth if we are to avoid the various dooms predicted for us. But if the nurturing instinct is so strongly hardwired into us, what happens when we ask people not to have so many kids? The role animals play in meeting this desperate vacuum should be obvious."

Researchers at Waltham revealed that while talking to other people, even loved ones, raises blood pressure, talking to or petting a dog lowers it. The effect is enhanced even more when talking to or petting your *own* dog. Elderly people who share their homes with pets make fewer visits to the doctor and report themselves to be happier than do non-pet-owning seniors. According to a report in the *Journal of the American Veterinary Medical Association*, elderly pet owners are also less likely to develop cancer.

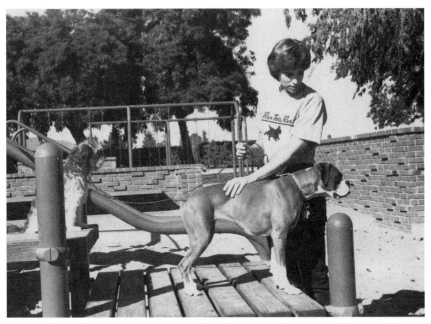

This handler offers a reassuring touch to her Boxer, who is concerned about the footing on the playground equipment.

In a survey of the CEOs of Fortune 500 companies, the majority credited having a pet during childhood with learning responsibility, discipline and, above all, empathy. More than 90 percent of them currently own a dog.

At the University of Pennsylvania, a long-term study of heart attack victims found that the first predictor of survival was the degree of heart damage suffered. The second most important factor was pet ownership, showing a greater effect than all other social, economic and physical variables. Those heart attack victims who owned dogs were found to be less depressed about their circumstances, more social and more active.

In their *Bodywork for Dogs* video, Lynn Vaughan and Deborah Jones note that effectively massaging a dog takes time and provides an opportunity for some silence and reflection. We all need some time every day to relax, unwind and recenter ourselves. Massage can deepen the connection between owner and dog and enhance trust and awareness, creating a much more profound relationship. Effective massage also relieves stress and tension, helping the dog to relax and think more clearly.

PHYSICAL BENEFITS OF TOUCH

Laboratory studies can demonstrate increased endorphin levels (those natural feel-good neurochemicals) and other neurochemical changes in response to slow relaxed touching. There's no question that kind touch has many benefits to offer.

Massaging your dog before strenuous activity can warm up muscles, increase flexibility and ready the body to perform—but you have to know your dog and how much to do. Some dogs become so relaxed that they are almost in a stupor, hardly ready to give their all. After the activity, a quick rubdown can help remove lactic acid from muscles and prevent cramps and stiffness.

You may have heard that dogs aren't particularly aware of where their hind legs and tail are. That's why they have to work at learning to negotiate an agility dog walk or, even harder, a ladder. Some seem better at it than others, but massage can increase a dog's awareness of all parts of her body.

Massage may also help dogs to recover from physical injury or surgery, but here you should proceed with caution. Dogs in compromised health can potentially be injured by massage if you don't know what you're doing. Dogs with fevers, for example, should definitely *not* be massaged because the increased blood flow can push the fever higher. Yet doing massage or TTouch correctly can speed healing and help prevent buildup of scar tissue. Consult with your veterinarian about receiving instruction to be sure your efforts are beneficial.

Think About It

In some states, the only people who can legally charge a fee to perform massage on your animal are veterinarians and licensed veterinary technicians. Massage is considered a form of veterinary medicine, and cannot be offered on animals by a massage therapist accredited for humans, or by those not accredited at all. You may think this unnecessarily restrictive, but it does provide some assurance that the masseur understands canine anatomy and psychology, and has some background in canine disease.

THOUGHTS ABOUT MASSAGE

Intent is an important factor in massage. Practitioners talk about "centering" themselves, and many advocate breathing exercises. As Bonnie Wilcox, DVM, says, "There's an energetic connection, whether the Western world wants to admit that or not. You don't want to be doing massage work and figuring out the fight you had with your spouse last night."

So before you even think about laying hands on your dog, you need to do a little work on yourself. If you've ever done any meditation, that can be helpful in quieting your mind. Sitting somewhere and simply slowing and deepening your breathing will have a great effect, and, in fact, most breathing exercises will serve you well even when you're not contemplating massage. Most people actually don't breathe very well or use much of their lung capacity. You may be surprised at an increase in your sense of well-being just from learning to breathe a bit better.

Most forms of massage are based in Eastern thought and the idea of the body as an energetic system. The energy of the body flows freely when the body is in good health and is blocked when there is sickness. This is not an easy concept for us Westerners to wrap our minds around.

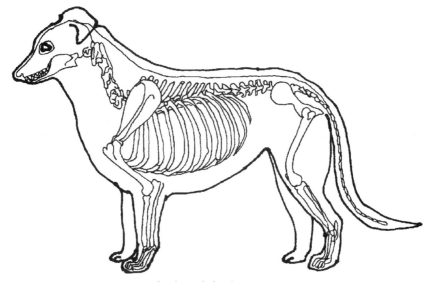

The dog's skeletal structure.

Try It Yourself

Here's an experiment that may help convince you. You'll need a second person to help you.

Stand up and hold one arm straight out to the side parallel with the floor. Have your assistant put a hand over the top of your wrist and press downward while you resist, pushing upward with your arm. Both of you notice how hard you're pushing.

Now have your helper say something uncomplimentary to you— you're stingy, have terrible taste, gained some weight, whatever— and immediately try the arm strength test again.

What happened?

Did your helper succeed in pushing your arm down, even though you tried your hardest to resist? The negative energy in the unkind words is usually enough to temporarily sap your strength.

Think about that and remember what you were probably told as a child—if you don't have anything nice to say, don't say anything at all.

One excellent piece of advice comes from Debra Potts, who says, "Always remember that we are doing this *with* the dog, not to the dog." By watching your dog's reactions, you will know when what you are doing is comforting and when you should try something else.

BASIC MASSAGE

Presuming that you have a healthy dog, some free time and are in a reasonably good mood, now might be a good time to try massage with your dog. Remember to pay attention to the responses you get from your dog. Understand that massage does *not* have to be forceful. A light touch is actually preferable—just enough to part the fur or to move the skin over the muscles, depending on where you are on the body and what massage stroke you are using.

If your dog has eaten recently, wait at least one hour before giving a massage. Don't use any of the lotions or oils sometimes used in human massage. In fact, be sure that your hands are freshly washed, then rub them together briskly until you feel heat or tingling, to get the energy flowing.

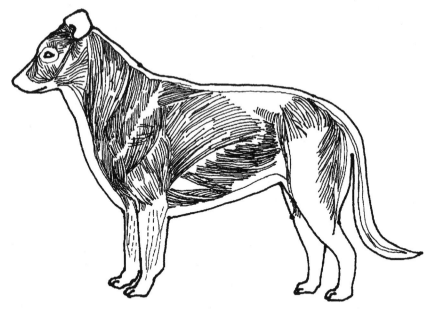

The dog's muscular structure.

Some Massage Techniques

You probably already *stroke* your dog, but did you realize that the speed and direction of your strokes can influence your dog's state of mind? Stroking uses the whole hand, with palms flat and fingers together, in a slow continuous motion over the dog's body. You will most often hear recommendations to stroke with the lay of the dog's coat. Slow, quiet stroking with the fur can soothe and quiet a dog, while faster firmer stroking against the lay of the fur can excite and stimulate a dog.

You might also hear about a whole-hand flowing stroke technique called *effleurage*. In *Canine Massage*, Jean-Pierre Hourdebaigt and Shari L. Seymour explain that stroking uses either the finger pads or the palms and can move along the muscles in either direction, while effleurage uses the whole hand and should always move toward the heart, "to assist the natural flow of the venous blood circulation."

Petrissage is the other major component of massage, comprised of a variety of techniques that lift, roll and squeeze the tissues. *Kneading* certainly fills this function, though different practitioners describe it differently. The video *Bodywork for Dogs* shows a massage therapist placing her hands around the dog's upper front leg, one from the front and one from the back, and alternating squeezing each hand over the muscles. Hourdebaigt and Seymour describe the stroke as rhythmic, done with the thumbs or pads of the first three fingers in a continuous line of small arcs, similar to the way you might knead bread dough. Feel free to experiment to find the technique that best suits you and your dog.

Skin rolling requires a light touch or it's likely to be annoying. Pick up the loose skin and roll it gently between the thumb and fingers. The direction of the rolling isn't important. The back of the neck just ahead of the shoulders is a good place to start because most dogs have a good amount of loose skin in this area.

Circles use the pads of two or three fingers. You push the skin over the muscles in small slow circles. You'll be hearing a lot more about circles in the next section, covering a different way of touching, Tellington Touch.

Vibrations are very fast but small movements of the hand, with the whole hand resting over a joint. The best I can describe it is to picture your elbow starting to shiver, then letting the movement flow down your forearm muscles and into your hand. Alternate vibrations with effleurage, and don't do vibrations on your dog's head.

Another form of touch therapy is *acupressure*, a technique that uses finger pressure on specific points of the body along the traditional energy pathways of Eastern medicine. Though some insist that you don't have to be able to locate the precise points to be effective, I advise against attempting acupressure on your dog unless you are trained. The points are very specific, vary in their location from individual to individual and have the potential for causing harm.

Something a lot of dog owners do instinctively for their dogs is *ear strokes*. Caressing those long, silky ears seems to be almost irresistible. Taking the ear between thumb and fingers and simply sliding from the base to the tip is both stimulating and safe, so long as you remember to keep a light touch. The ears are full of acupressure points, and the majority of dogs enjoy having their ears stroked. (You'll read more on touching the ears in the section on Tellington Touch.)

You Can Quote Me

Touch is very very important to build a better bond. The classic example I see is in birds. People who handle their birds on a regular basis, get them out and pet them and feed them little things, have birds who are easy to handle. Cats who are never handled, they're just no fun to examine because every time you touch them they're in the flight or fight syndrome and there's going to be blood all over the room, and it's not going to be the cat's.

Dennis Wilcox, D.V.M.

Tapotement is a less well-known term, though one of its forms is what many people picture when they think of massage. Tapotement consists of soft rhythmic blows to the body. *Hacking*, done with the outside edges of the hands, is the technique commonly depicted when massage is shown in movies or on television. There are also two versions of tapotement using the palms—*clapping* with the hands flat and *cupping* with the hands curved so that they would form a rough sphere if you brought them together.

Finally, *stretching* or passive exercise can be useful if your dog is cooperative and you are very careful. With the dog lying on her side, grasp and support the exposed front leg and gently move it forward. Hold it there for a few seconds, then move it back and hold, then return it to its resting position. Do the same with the rear leg. Do not push beyond the slightest sign of resistance. This exercise should not be uncomfortable for your dog.

There are other variations of canine massage, but these will give you a fairly extensive repertoire and are relatively safe and easy to learn.

Your Massage Routine

There are probably as many ways to combine these techniques as there are people practicing massage. A good strategy concentrates first on relaxing yourself and your dog, especially if you are both new at this.

For yourself, do some general stretching to try and get rid of some of your own tension. Then sit on the floor with your dog and take some slow deep breaths. When you feel calm and centered, you're ready to begin.

Have the dog lie down in front of you. If she will lie on her side, that's perfect, but if she'd rather be upright, let her be. You don't want to start out with a struggle.

Start with some general whole-hand stroking. Slowly let your hands travel all over the dog's body, trying to sense any spots that seem warmer or cooler and any tension. Note any reactions from your dog. You are helping her to relax while looking for any potential trouble spots. If your dog is athletic, you should particularly heed any knots in the muscles. These trigger points can be quite sensitive, and careful work may help loosen them. Remember to keep your breathing slow and relaxed as you move your hands over your dog.

Resting your hands gently on the dog, move to the back of her neck. Using kneading, skin rolling or circles (whatever seems best to you), work slowly around the base of the ear (both ears if your dog is upright) and down to the tops of the shoulders. At some point your dog may close her eyes, sigh, take an extra-deep breath or seem to soften and melt under your hands. These are all good signs of relaxation.

Most massage therapists recommend next working down the back. Remember, you don't need to work directly over the vertebrae, but just to the side, where you're dealing with skin and muscle rather than skin and bone. Circles, skin rolling and stroking can all work here. If your dog doesn't enjoy this, you're probably pressing too hard. Lighten up, literally.

When you get to the end of your dog's back, massage all around the base of her tail, then slowly work your way down the tail, using two hands and gently bending each individual joint in the tail, all the way out to the tip. Walk your hands back up the tail again, and massage over the hip area. Feel for tension—dogs are often tense either in their neck or hip areas. Try several techniques over the hip to see which ones the dog seems to enjoy.

Walk your hands back up to the ears, and this time keep going past them, to the face. Stroke the head, over the eyes and down the muzzle. Do some gentle kneading over the sides of the face in back of the mouth.

Work down the front of the neck and chest, being careful not to press on the trachea. Most dogs calm beautifully if you slowly stroke down one side of the breastbone, so if your dog doesn't seem completely relaxed, work in this area for a while. Be sure to go all the way down under the front leg, so this section isn't neglected.

This clever little keychain includes a comb just large enough to provide some skin-tingling brushing.

Move to the shoulder area, where you're working with muscle attachments over a large bone. The rule is to be firmer where you're over muscle and gentler where you're over bone. Alternate kneading with stroking, and be sure to cover the entire area, as many muscles run through this part of the dog. When the shoulder feels warm and relaxed to you, gradually work down the leg. Place your hands around the leg, one from the front and one from the back, as high on the shoulder as you can get. Squeeze alternately with each hand. Work slowly down to the elbow, lightening up over the joint. Picture the elbow joint as a hinge, and move the leg so that you open and close the hinge several times. Continue massaging down to the wrist, then open and close the wrist several times. Cover the whole foot with your hand and squeeze gently. Stroke up the inside and outside of the leg, remembering to keep at least one hand always in contact with the dog.

Now work the rib cage. Stroke down from the spine toward the chest, letting your fingers find the soft grooves between the ribs. Starting from just behind the shoulder, work your way back to the last rib. Knead, circle or stroke up the belly to the chest under the foreleg, then come back across the rib cage to the last rib and work over the loin area, behind the ribs. Warming and loosening the loin can help strengthen the hind legs and is especially helpful for arthritic older dogs, large-breed puppies going through growth spurts or dogs with hip dysplasia. From the loin, move to the hind leg, encircling it with both hands. Work as you did with the front leg, kneading as you travel down it, opening and closing the joints and ending by squeezing the foot.

When you're finished with the hind leg, walk your hands back up to the head. You'll finish this side with an almost continuous sweep over your dog's body, stroking from the tip of the muzzle to the neck, down the neck to the chest, up to the shoulders and down the front leg, then down the back and ribs, over the loin, down the hind leg and out to the end of the tail. Now you're ready to turn the dog over and do the other side.

This is only a superficial introduction aimed at getting you started. If you're interested in learning more about massaging your dog, check out the Resources section. Of course, if you can get some face-to-face guidance from an experienced licensed canine massage therapist, that would be best of all. Just remember that a light touch can be very effective, but a heavy touch can be harmful. Above all, listen to your dog.

TELLINGTON TOUCH

Background

Linda Tellington-Jones, an animal touch expert, developed a different, very specific method of canine massage. A long-time equestrian enthusiast, Linda and her then-husband Wentworth Tellington published the first paper about using massage on horses to speed recovery after endurance rides.

In the 1970s, Linda conducted clinics in Germany that dealt with problem horses while studying as a Feldenkrais practitioner. The Feldenkrais method teaches humans Awareness Through Movement (with an instructor verbally guiding the subject through a sequence of movements), and Functional Integration (where the movement guidance is hands-on). The originator was a Russian physicist, mechanical engineer and practitioner of judo. Finding the Feldenkrais method of massage difficult to learn, even after four years of study, Tellington-Jones developed the circular touch that now bears her name. She first unveiled the method she called TTEAM in 1978, and published a book about it soon afterward. TTEAM originally stood for Tellington-Jones Equine Awareness Method, but Tellington-Jones eventually changed the name to Tellington-Jones Every Animal Method, since it came to be used outside the world of horses. It is sometimes known as Tellington Touch or TTouch.

As she further developed the technique, Tellington-Jones added the slow, rhythmic breathing typical of massage, and a scale of pressure for the touches, ranging from 1 to 9. She insists that TTouch is *not* a form of massage. In *The Tellington Touch for Cats and Kittens*, she explains, "Massage is done with the intent of affecting the muscular system; the intent of TTouch is the reorganizing of the nervous system and activating the function of the cells." Tellington-Jones claims

Dogs are eminently touchable.

that TTouch increases an animal's self-image and awareness and says there is no need to know anatomy because using the TTouch anywhere on the body improves health and awareness. She terms it a very special interspecies nonverbal communication.

Tellington-Jones postulates that problems between humans and animals arise out of lack of understanding, or habitual or instinctive responses to pain or the fear of pain. The Tellington method attempts to break through these automatic reactions and teach new patterns. Whether that's actually happening or not, kind touch is generally beneficial to the human-dog relationship, and TTouch provides pleasant, relaxing touch.

The TTouch Technique

The most often discussed part of the TTouch technique is the circular touches, moving from what would be 6 o'clock on a traditional clock face, clockwise for one full circle plus enough extra to take you to approximately 8 o'clock. A variety of hand positions are used. A flat whole-hand touch is called the Abalone, with the hand conforming to the shape of the body. A touch with the fingers bent slightly, the thumb serving as an anchor and the pads of the fingers making the circles, is called the Clouded Leopard. A less often used touch using just the fingertips is called the Raccoon.

Debra Potts, an early practitioner of TTouch, notes, "Circles should be round. If your hands are tense, you won't make good circles. And if your wrist or arm gets sore, you're doing something wrong." The fingers or hand should move the skin, not slide over it. If you find your hand sliding, you're probably making your circles too big. To get a feel for how much pressure to use, do circles on your own eyelid. You can practice on your own arm or leg, noting how much pressure is needed and how it feels when your circles are smooth. When working with an animal, one hand does the circles while the other hand just rests on the body, providing a physical connection.

TTouch also includes motions other than circles. The Python lift uses either the flat hand or the finger pads to lift the skin away from the direction of gravity. Hold it there a second, then slowly lower it back down. The lift can be done on its own or at the finish of a circle. Slides are most often done on the ears, placing the thumb on one surface and some or all of the fingers on the other side, starting at the connection to the head and gliding with light pressure to the tip.

You may find it helpful initially to practice on humans so that they can give you verbal feedback about your efforts. Though other people won't be exactly the same as your dog, they can tell you if you're pressing too hard or not completing your circles or not making them round. And you should also find someone to practice on you, so you know what it feels like to be on the receiving end.

Begin with a flat-hand, long stroking movement that TTouch calls Noah's march. This serves to make a connection between you and the subject and lets you gather information such as warm or cool spots, differences in the haircoat and any places where the subject is reluctant to be touched.

Start with circles in a location likely to be pleasant—a person's back or a dog's shoulders often make good choices. Picture your starting point (6 o'clock) oriented either toward the dog's feet or her tail. Do one circular movement in a location, then slide your hand to another location and do another circle movement. *Where* you do the circles is said to be largely unimportant, which negates the need for a basic understanding of anatomy. TTouch practitioners advise just instinctively letting your hand make circles where it will. But they also advise to watch your dog's reaction, and to change what you're doing if the dog appears restless or uncomfortable or eager to get away from you. Don't put your dog on a command such as "down stay" while you do TTouch work. The dog should feel free to move so you can assess how your efforts are being received.

Ear work is often recommended. While TTouch practitioners don't use acupressure points, they acknowledge that the ears are full of them and thus touches on the ears can produce major results in the body. You can use slides, small circles and also move the entire ear in circles. According to TTouch, work on the ears assists in physical and emotional balance.

The somewhat more controversial area recommended by TTouch practitioners is the mouth. They say that mouth work is good for stress, nervousness, hyperactivity, emotional upset, barking, chewing and aggression. Some behaviorists take issue with telling people to poke their hands in the mouths of aggressive or biting dogs.

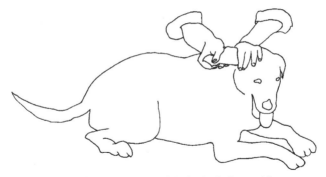

Ear slides often prove enjoyable for both dog and human.

If you think your dog is trustworthy and want to try this work, sit behind your dog and support the dog's chin with one hand. Do *not* wrap your hand around the muzzle and hold on—the dog definitely won't like that. Stroke down the side of the mouth with your free hand and do small circles, using the same pressure you would use on your eyelids. Watch your dog's reactions carefully.

According to TTouch theory, dogs often carry fear in their hindquarters and tails, so work in these areas can be helpful. You can use circles and lifts over the haunches and circles on the legs, but work the tail differently. Gently bend each joint of the tail, working your way out from the body. Then bend larger sections, curving the tail in all directions. How you do this will of course depend on how much tail your dog has, but for dogs with cropped tails, Potts advises working beyond the existing tail into the space where the tail would be had it not been shortened. Do a modified lift, gently pulling the tail away from the body, holding for a second, then slowly relaxing. You can also do circles the length of the tail.

In all TTouch work, it's important to remember to breathe. People new to this technique tend to hold their breath while they concentrate on making circles, but holding your breath tenses the body. So think about slow, regular breathing while you work. If you can only do three or four circles at first before you tense up, that's fine. Potts says that TTouch affects the subject's nervous system, and the body continues processing information from the touches for 24 hours afterward, so a little work can go a long way. If you are in doubt about any part of doing TTouch, Potts advises that a good general

You Can Quote Me

There are powerful correlations between body posture, breathing patterns, facial expressions, and emotional states. Body language is all about the *outward* expression of *internal* physiological states.

Suzanne Clothier, *Body Posture & Emotions*

rule is "less is more"—less pressure, less repetition, a less sensitive location.

At the finish of working circles, long flowing touches all across the animal's body complete the treatment.

OTHER TOUCH WORK

I mentioned trigger points earlier in this chapter. These tight knots within muscles can benefit from some vigorous massage work. But you have to be careful to make a correct identification of the swelling or lump. Vigorously massaging a cyst or an abscess is not going to be helpful and could actually be harmful.

Finally, some behaviorists (notably, Suzanne Clothier and Ian Dunbar) recommend changing a dog's posture to help change the dog's emotions.

Clothier describes how she worked with a frightened dog, gently stroking her under the stomach to encourage her to stand taller and massaging the flattened ears to help them loosen. We'll look at the mind-body connection further in Chapter 10, X-tra Sensory. For now, realize that touch means a lot to most animals, including ourselves, and that *how* you touch can have a definite impact. And don't think you're only influencing the dog. If you think about it, you'll find that your own breathing slows and your body relaxes as you do this work. The benefits flow both ways.

CHAPTER 9

Kids Speaking Canine

What should kids know about interacting with dogs?
What should dogs know about interacting with kids?

Something in us turns toward that which is genuine, like a
flower turns toward the light. A dog never gives less than one
hundred percent of himself. Can you imagine humans doing
this? If they would, a transformation would come over the
entire world.

J. Allen Boone

*This coyote story, told in different forms by various native peoples, explains why
dogs sniff each other the way they do.*

*Long ago, near the time of creation, the Dog People met to have a celebra-
tion. They danced and ran and sang and played all day and late into the night.
Coyote tried to join in, but the Dog People would not accept him, saying he was
too mangy and sneaky to be a real dog.*

*At last, all the dogs went inside, hung up their tails, lay down and went
right to sleep. Coyote, angry at having been excluded, played a trick. He placed
some smoldering logs near the dwelling so the dogs would smell the smoke, then
ran around yelling, "Fire! Fire!"*

*The dogs awoke in the darkness. They smelled the smoke and heard the
yelling and thought they were in danger of being burned up. They all leaped up,
grabbed a tail at random and ran out into the night. When they understood the
trick Coyote had played on them, they chased after Coyote. Some stopped after a
short while, but others kept going, scattering dogs all over the world.*

*By the time the dogs realized that they did not have their own tails, they were
too spread out to meet and have a group exchange. So ever since, when dogs meet
one another, they sniff each other's tails, trying to find the one they lost so long ago.*

Sooner or later, most parents will have to face the question "Can I have a dog?" What could be more natural than kids and dogs together? In fact, in her book *Canine Behavior: A Guide for Veterinarians*, Bonnie Beaver reports that the most common reason given for dog ownership is the presence of a child in the household. However, since more than 60 percent of those bitten by dogs are children, both the child and the dog need training and supervision to ensure that both are safe and happy.

THE ADVANTAGES OF DOG-OWNING CHILDREN

A dog confers many instant advantages on a child. Dogs are attractive to most children, so a child who has a dog becomes more attractive by association. In the often-cruel world of childhood, such an ice-breaker can be invaluable. Those active in the realm of the physically challenged know well that while a child in a wheelchair may seem "different," unapproachable and even slightly scary, a child in a wheel-chair with a canine companion is seen by other kids as a sort of different kid who has a dog. The possibilities for social interaction increase, so much so that some dogs who accompany such children are not service dogs in the usual sense—they don't pick up dropped items or pull the wheelchair from place to place. They're social facilitator dogs, there simply to make the "different" child more socially acceptable to his or her peers.

This phenomenon isn't confined to the disabled. Children in general with dogs in the home tend to have more visits from classmates and to be more popular. In fact, some classrooms have taken to keeping a canine mascot in the room, often the teacher's own dog. One study found that when a pet was part of the class setting, self-esteem scores increased significantly over one school year. Even more encouragingly, those children who initially had the lowest scores showed the most substantial improvement.

A dog also offers a kind and nonjudgmental ear that's always available to listen to problems and heartaches, and a warm furry body to snuggle up to. The advantages conferred on a child by a dog not only help make the turbulent years of youth more pleasant, but last well into adulthoood. Remember the Fortune 500 CEOs I mentioned in the last chapter? They credit their childhood pets with

Think About It

Think back to when you were feeling low or upset and took your problems to your best friend, the one you can always confide in. Did he or she give you some wise, earth-shattering advice that made everything right with the world? Probably not. What that friend probably did was to listen, make sympathetic sounds and maybe offer a hug or two, all of which falls well within the capabilities of the average dog. Their eyes exude sympathy and understanding, their touch is warm and soft and they *never* gossip. Psychologist Boris Levinson was one of the first to realize that his dog, who accompanied him to the office, could be as effective a therapist as himself, encouraging clients to talk about problems while accepting the friendship of another being. And dogs don't even charge for their services.

teaching them the responsibility and discipline required in their high-powered adult lives. A measure of their self-confidence probably derived from their pets as well. Nearly all of them continue to be dog owners in their adult lives.

In fact, the benefits of pet ownership extend to the entire family. A survey found that 70 percent of pet-owning families reported an increased sense of fun and even greater happiness as a direct result of getting a pet. Interaction among family members increased, and both adults and children felt that the pets were sensitive to their moods and emotional well-being.

A dog rarely has anything more important to do than play with a child. In this often hectic world, this can be a godsend, but it can also be a problem, depending on the age and maturity of the child. Remember those dog bite statistics. The vast majority result from family or neighborhood pets, *not* from strange dogs roaming loose.

PROMOTING SAFETY FOR CHILDREN AROUND DOGS

Regardless of all the positive aspects of owning a dog, parents should not give in to requests for a dog, no matter how urgent, without carefully thinking the matter through. While children can toss aside a game or toy a month later with nothing more than a monetary sense of loss, a dog cannot be likewise discarded. Even if a child swears to be totally responsible for the dog, it won't happen. Parents will need to see to veterinary care, licensing and training, even if the child is as diligent as promised about feeding, exercising and playing with the dog. Often, even feeding and walking the dog will soon become the parent's tasks as the child loses interest. So it's essential that the entire family wants a dog. Anything less will likely result in strife over dog-related chores. The dog will often be relegated to the backyard, where she will be lonely, neglected and miserable.

Having a child and a dog in the family definitely requires more work. Trainer Mandy Book characterized the adult responsibility as "Supervise. Supervise. Supervise. Oh, did I mention supervise? And don't forget to supervise. Work on possession and food bowl exercises. Teach the dog to enjoy rough handling and screaming, really *like* it. Give the dog a place to go, when it gets too much, where the child can't follow. Don't ever assume there won't be a problem. Don't ever assume the dog will grow out of a problem. And oh yeah, supervise."

Book is facetious to make a point: Lack of supervision can result in a dog bite. Nearly all those reports of family dogs who "bite without warning" are actually reports of families who failed to observe the warning signs. So, the first safety tip is that the family must be ready to welcome a dog into its midst, and willing to give the time to make the dog a worthwhile family member.

Choice of dog may be important, depending somewhat on the child's age. Keep in mind that generalizations are just that, and that no matter what breed characteristics you may read, each dog is an individual. A breed noted for even temper and gentleness can still include aggressive individuals, just as a highly reactive feisty breed can have calm and laid-back members. Keep in mind that the following observations are general in nature and should neither condemn nor sanctify a breed.

Although Cocker Spaniels have been popular family dogs for many years, in many studies they are the number one breed for dog bites, and nearly always bite family members. Other studies rank Chihuahuas as number one. Terriers in general can be active and easily aroused and may bite without any ill intent. Herding dogs may nip in an attempt to corral children into a manageable flock.

Many of the breeds recommended for families are part of the Hound and Sporting Groups. Golden Retrievers have often been called the perfect dog for children, but as they became more popular, incidents of aggression have risen. Labrador Retrievers are often touted as good family dogs, although some familiar with the breed say to stay away from the chocolate variety and others caution to avoid hunting lines. Newfoundlands and Old English Sheepdogs have been popularized as "nannies," and can be considered generally reliable (but large enough to knock over small children merely by turning around). Bloodhounds, Basset Hounds and Bulldogs are all recommended for their equanimity. And don't discount mixed breeds. While you may not be able to predict exactly what the coat will look like or precisely how much she'll weigh when fully grown, you can conduct the same sort of temperament check with a mixed breed that you can with a purebred.

Whatever dog you bring into the home (we'll talk about how to make your selection later in this chapter), you need to do all you can to accustom her to the sometimes annoying attentions of children.

Many problems arise around food bowls, so you should work to avoid them. Make a game out of dropping little tasty tidbits into the bowl while the dog is eating. If it's not an issue, pick the bowl up, add some extra treats and give it back to the dog. When you have done some obedience work, have the dog sit and stay while you put the bowl down. Children should not bother dogs while they are eating, but in case they do, you don't want the dog to turn instantly into a slavering beast bent on defending her meal.

Families with children can become quite loud at times. While it's certainly understandable for dogs to react to sudden loud noises, they shouldn't take it out on the noisemaker or whoever happens to be standing closest to them at the time. The best family dogs can sleep right through the usual family background noise. If yelling is your family's style, have family members shout back and forth to each other while you feed the dog some cookies.

Children also move in short jerky bursts and often flail their arms around. This is a tough one for dogs. Such erratic movement triggers their prey instinct and makes them want to chase and grab. Acting on such impulses can be the last mistake a dog will be allowed to make.

You can tell young people not to behave like this around dogs, and perhaps your own children might even listen, but their friends probably won't, so you need to teach the dog how to behave in such circumstances.

The urge to chase can be very strong, and you probably won't be able to banish it entirely. Instead, provide the dog with an acceptable outlet. Teach the dog to chase and fetch tennis balls. Control access to these toys and only bring them out to play the chase game. Then start having your children play nearby while you play with the dog. Next, have the chase toy out on the ground when your youngsters start running and jumping around, and encourage the dog to get the toy so that you can play the game. The association should become automatic, so that when things start getting wild, the dog looks for a

COURTESY OF THE WALTHAM CENTRE FOR PET NUTRITION

Teach both child and dog how to behave around food.

You Can Quote Me

Supervise is always a hint, but you have to let people know what that means. It doesn't mean that you're upstairs on your computer while the kid is downstairs beating the dog over the head with his toy. You have to spell that out. But even with true supervision, it can be nearly impossible. I was with one of my best friends and her little boy, and this kid's been raised around horses and Akitas and cats. He was maybe 18 months of age and sitting on the sofa next to my Maggie, the world's most perfect dog, and he had Maggie's brush and was gently brushing her. His mom was sitting on one side and I was sitting on the other, and we were both looking at him, and he turned the brush over and hit Maggie on the head. There was nothing we were going to be able to do to anticipate that—we're already doing it! They're just trying these things out. And what I learned from that is Maggie was an extraordinary dog, and I don't have a dog in my household now that I would let be around a kid that age, no matter what the supervision.

Karen Overall

toy to grab. A dog with a toy in her mouth can't be biting anything else. You are responsible for ensuring that the toy is available to the dog in circumstances where she may need it.

Most police dogs are rewarded at the end of drug searches or criminal apprehensions with the chance to play with their ball or a rolled-up towel. It's a potent motivator and can avoid otherwise deadly problems.

Teach your children how to behave when meeting dogs (which we'll cover in the next section), then take them somewhere that will provide encounters with plenty of dogs, such as an obedience trial. Watching how closely your children adhere to what they've been taught will give you a good idea of their level of control. Seeing all those dogs is pretty exciting—don't be surprised if everything you thought they'd learned falls by the wayside. It just means they're not ready yet and you have more training to do.

If there's already a dog in the home when children arrive, then it is up to you to make that dog as "bombproof" as possible (meaning that nothing within the bounds of reason will set the dog off). It also falls to you to manage circumstances at all times so that neither child nor dog is put in a situation of potentially losing control.

THE TRAINING PROGRAM FOR CHILDREN

Even if you don't have a dog in your home, there are plenty of them outside your door. If your child is frustrated in trying to get a dog into the household, he or she will be that much more eager to meet any dogs that present themselves. Teaching the child how to meet dogs is both essential to safety and a good indication of the child's level of control.

If a dog is in the company of humans, children should first politely ask permission to pet the dog. If the human says no for whatever reason, that's the end of the matter. (The dog may not get along with children, the owner may be afraid of liability issues or the dog may just have been brushed for the show ring.)

If the human says yes, the child should extend a hand for the dog to sniff. This is a friendly gesture, akin to a human handshake, and avoids startling the dog with a sudden pat on the head.

Once the dog has sniffed the hand, the child may pet the dog. The front of the chest or anywhere along the sides of the body will generally meet with the dog's favor. Some dogs feel intimidated by a hand going over their heads, so the top of the head is best left alone. (Children seem to have a tendency to want to pound rather than to pet here anyway— another reason to teach them not the touch the dog's head.)

Unknown dogs should not be hugged. While you can desensitize your own dog into accepting, even enjoying, this gesture, other dogs may not tolerate it well. Being restrained in such a fashion may raise the automatic "fight or flight" response in the dog.

Children should not stare at dogs. Though this may be natural behavior in human children, it is impolite and potentially challenging in canine parlance. Stable, well-behaved dogs will recognize the lack of ill intentions, but other dogs may not. Teach children to play a game of looking at dogs out of the corners of their eyes.

Impress upon children that they should move more slowly around dogs and should speak more quietly. Tell them that wild dogs have to

Children should never approach unaccompanied dogs, even nice-looking ones like this.

hunt to eat and that the easiest things for them to hunt are injured animals, which is what kids look like to dogs when they jerk their arms around and move in fits and starts. The child needs to help the dog recognize him or her as a small human.

When encountering unaccompanied dogs, a child's behavior is even more critical. Children should *never* initiate contact with dogs on their own, even if they know the dogs. A dog behind a fence in her yard may act quite differently from one out for a walk with a member of the household. Or the dog may be suffering an ear mite infestation and be very reactive to being touched on the head. For any number of reasons, dogs alone are best left alone.

If an unsupervised dog approaches a child, the child should stand still, avoid eye contact and in a whisper, as if telling a secret to a good friend, recite a nursery rhyme or a song or anything that comes to mind. Quiet rhythmic talking can have a calming effect on both the child and the dog. This is not a natural reaction for an adult human in such a situation, let alone a child, so the idea must be planted deeply. You can practice when you're out with a child and you see someone walking a dog. Have the child demonstrate the aforementioned stranger dog safety response, and reward him or her with being allowed to pet the dog (with the dog owner's permission, of course).

When on her own, a child should stay in the safety posture for a few moments, then if the unsupervised dog is not approaching, back slowly away. Children should never run within sight of a strange dog. The first dog bite I ever received, at the age of seven or eight, was in the back of the leg from a very nice young dog who simply couldn't resist chasing and grabbing when I ran.

If the dog does approach and seems aggressive or is growling or barking, trying to edge away may inspire an attack. If adults are in the area, a single shout for help may bring some assistance without setting off the dog. Shouting brings its own risks, however, and should be reserved for serious situations. Holding something as seemingly insignificant as a sheet of paper or a notebook between you and the dog may direct the dog's attention to the object rather than to you. Back away while holding the object out in front of you.

Children must understand not to bother dogs that are eating or in possession of some object they may not want to relinquish. While the rules for dogs (in the next section) within the household are that no objects, including food bowls, are guarded, outside dogs aren't subject to these rules. Children also should not disturb dogs who are sleeping. The phrase "let sleeping dogs lie" has good safety sense behind it, because a dog who is awakened suddenly may be startled into defensive behavior.

Under no circumstances should a child hit, poke or prod a dog. Those looking for trouble are likely to find it.

If you approach all of this in a calm, matter-of-fact manner and present these techniques as the proper way to converse with canines, you can educate a child without going overboard and making him or her afraid of dogs.

THE TRAINING PROGRAM FOR DOGS

Just like everyone else in the family, the dog should have a place where she can go when she doesn't want to be disturbed. This might be a roomy open-door crate or a laundry room. Whatever area you use, children must understand that when the dog is in "her room," she must not be bothered. Relate the dog's special space to the children's own rooms, and remind them that they don't want people just bursting into their private space all the time. If you see the dog starting to get stressed, take the dog to her place, offer a toy or a chew and leave her there to calm down (but free to come out when she wants). The dog will soon learn she can go there on her own.

If the dog has access to the yard, make sure that she won't be at the mercy of passing children. Dogs behind fences tend to be a little more guarded about who can come near them, and some children, usually boys, can't seem to resist trying to get the dog to bark and lunge at the fence. By fencing a dog yard within the outer fence, you provide a buffer zone for the dog and remove most of the temptation.

Do not tie a dog in an unfenced yard. That frustrates the dog and leaves her an unprotected target for teasing. If you must restrain a dog without a fence, at least use an overhead cable runner so that the dog has more freedom of movement. Bear in mind, however, that a great percentage of dog bites to children are inflicted by tied-out dogs.

It doesn't matter whether you adopt a puppy or an adult dog; you must gently and gradually accustom the dog to as many people, places and situations as possible. Being used to children is certainly a major socialization issue. Even if you don't have children in your household, you should still take the time to introduce children to your dog. Not all parents teach their children to approach dogs slowly and ask permission before petting. Sooner or later you will probably see a child running toward your dog yelling, "Puppy, puppy!" and flailing and grabbing at the dog. If your dog has had no experience with such behavior, there's no telling what her reaction will be. All dogs should be accustomed to being handled in ways typical of children—hugs around the neck and tugs on ears and tails—and the sights and sounds of children at large.

After your new dog has had a few days to settle into your household, start inviting people over. Don't have a party for a hundred guests, but have two to five people at a time. Try for as much variety as possible—men, women, children, tall, short, boisterous, refined, with beards, hats or glasses. Enlist the services of your mail carrier or package delivery person if you can. If they take time now to introduce themselves and provide a few treats and pats, it could prevent the dog from barking at these people for the next 10 or 15 years! This also allows your dog to get used to seeing people in uniform, a subtle nicety that dogs recognize quite readily.

It's best not to force people on your dog, but simply have the dog in the room and let her make the approach. Give your guests treats they can use to reward the dog when she initiates friendly contact. Gradually let kids behave more like kids so that the dog gets used to shrill voices and spastic movement.

If you find that your dog does not react well to children and doesn't seem to be improving over time, you will need to manage such encounters for the life of the dog. My newest dog, Nestle, a shelter adoption, showed me almost immediately that young boys drove him wild. Just seeing boys running and playing in the distance was enough to start him leaping in the air and screaming. I enlisted my nephews to start on desensitization, and we got Nestle calmed down, but he still does not trust or accept the advances of boys he doesn't know. I've taught him to come to me and let me handle the matter if a boy approaches him. Part of our pet therapy visits consists of doing tricks for the children in day care at the convalescent center we visit, with the children safely behind a fence.

Nestle will probably never like young male children—he may have reason, given that most of his facial whiskers were cut off and one ear bore the imprint of human teeth when I got him. As long as I'm with him, his response is safe and reliable, and I'll never put him in the position of being around children without me present.

Even these kinds of problems can be managed, but it's best to see that they don't arise in the first place.

Puppies need to stay with their mothers and littermates until at least 8 weeks and preferably 12 weeks of age. They receive nearly all of their training in how to communicate with and act around other dogs during this period of life. Dog trainers are discovering a connection between puppies leaving their litters too soon and all sorts of behavioral problems later in life. The breeder of the litter should be taking care of early socialization during these first dozen weeks, too, so that puppies are eager to explore the world when they go to their new homes.

This is the ideal situation, of course, and not always the one with which you'll be dealing. Even without this excellent start in life, though, you can help your dog to learn the three basic skills that will see her safely through life—be slow to react, be quick to recover and inhibit any bite.

Be Slow to React

Even a sensitive dog will eventually learn to ignore incidents that at first catapulted her to the ceiling or unleashed a volley of barking. For sound-sensitive dogs, you can buy sound effect tapes of thunder, sirens and so on to acclimate her to noise. Start with the sound low enough so that the dog doesn't react, and gradually increase the volume over days and weeks.

Touch-sensitive dogs can also adapt to their situations. If your dog is averse to only certain parts her body being touched (many dogs don't like their feet handled, or object to having the fringe on their hind legs brushed), you can pet the dog in places she does enjoy, sneak in a touch to the "forbidden" area and then go directly back to the enjoyable petting. After a while, you will be able to touch the off-limits place for a little longer. Terry Ryan suggests what she calls "peanut butter therapy" for dogs who are sensitive about being brushed in certain areas. You smear some peanut butter on the refrigerator at dog height and let the dog lick it off while you gently brush the problem area for just a few seconds at first, gradually extending the time. Be aware that if the dog dislikes brushing more than she likes peanut butter, you can create a dog who can't be brushed and doesn't like peanut butter. Most touch-sensitivity is simply a lack of experience with kind touch. You can usually change the dog's mind about such issues simply by being patient and gentle.

Movement-oriented dogs, such as sighthounds, terriers and herding dogs, have to learn not to react instinctively to movement. Sighthounds have been known to kill small pets with whom they live, not because they don't like them, but because their instinct to chase and grab is triggered by the small animal running by. Many terriers were bred to hunt vermin and go into a frenzy when they see squirrels or other small critters. Herding dogs are more likely to nip than to truly bite, but they can also be easily triggered at the sight of a "stray" that needs to be rounded up. More than one Border Collie owner has returned from the kitchen with a fresh tray of appetizers

Both boy and dog seem used to the many sights and sounds of a dog show.

for the party only to find her guests huddled in the center of the room with the dog circling them. With these dogs, it helps to teach them an alternate way to react, such as grabbing one of her toys after spotting something exciting and bringing it to you for the cue to play a rousing game of tug, or coming to sit next to you for treats and a calming talk.

Be Quick to Recover

This idea is closely related to the previous section, because part of desensitization means learning to recover from a shock. People inadvertently cause problems in this area because they want to comfort a dog in distress. Petting and talking soothingly to an anxious dog may seem like a proper response to you, but the dog may read it as a reward for her behavior at the time. So petting your shaking dog after a clap of thunder may actually encourage the dog to shake harder and longer. Remember, the dog reads your actions, not your intentions.

A more beneficial response is to find some way to halt the reaction. Have the dog do some basic behaviors to get her mind focused on something else. Be upbeat and calm and ignore the trembling. Puppy instructors call it the "jolly routine." Instead of agreeing with the dog that the world may be coming to an end, you sound like a party's about to start. You may want to use a phrase that will come to mean everything's all right now, such as, "Ooh, that was scary." When the dog startles at some loud noise, if you say your phrase and then move happily on to other things, the phrase will become a reassurance that you're on top of things and life goes on despite occasional upsets (assuming that nothing bad actually happens to the dog after you've assured her everything's fine).

Practicing jazzing your dog up and then settling her down is a very useful exercise, and gives you another excellent communication term—*settle.*

With the dog on leash (so she doesn't go completely wild and decide to play keep-away with you), play fetch or tug or some other exciting game. Then bring the dog next to you, stroke gently down the side of the breastbone with one or two fingers and say "settle" in a low quiet voice. Make everything about your movements slow and hypnotic. You will have to work a bit to calm some dogs, but many will quiet right down. Eventually the word "settle" alone will be enough.

Being able to help your dog calm down can be very useful, but does require that you first be able to keep yourself calm. Saying "settle" while you are anxious and acting agitated isn't likely to have the desired effect.

Inhibit a Bite

If puppy stayed with her litter for a suitable length of time, her littermates and mother have already laid the groundwork for bite inhibition. Biting too hard during play brings yelping protests from littermates and a stop to the play (and possibly a reprimand from mother). Puppies learn to be a little softer with their mouths even when roughhousing.

Puppies from singleton litters or who were taken from their littermates too early may not have had this early experience and will be harder to work with. But persevere. The results are well worth it.

This dog's "bite" is the only good kind, putting money away for a rainy day.

The majority of dogs will respond to the same reaction they got from their littermates. If your dog bears down on your body with any mouth pressure, go ahead and yelp. Make it loud and high-pitched. Follow it up by turning your back on the dog and giving him the cold shoulder. You should use this response for gentler and gentler "bites." You want the dog to think that humans are very delicate and cannot withstand even the tiniest nip. If you can instill this thought deep inside your dog, it gives an extra layer of protection. If the dog ever does start to bite—and we're talking here about overexuberant play, not situations in which the dog feels that her life is in danger—she will be more likely to hold back and damage will be avoided or will be minimal.

I have met a few dogs who don't respond properly to the yelp. Some even think it's all part of the fun. They probably lacked early dog-to-dog socialization. You will have to work harder to teach them

---

 Think About It

Humans are often astonished when their happy-go-lucky, tail-wagging friend suddenly becomes a snarling, teeth-baring fiend over a scrap of rawhide or nearly empty food bowl. They shouldn't be. For dogs, possession isn't just nine-tenths of the law, it's ten-tenths of survival. Some dogs are so comfortable in their civilized surroundings that they can cast a beneficent eye on anyone meddling with their things. Others have been trained to view it as a good thing. But many regard the law of the jungle as still in effect.

manners. Have your dog on leash. If the dog puts her mouth on you, calmly pick up the leash and hook it around a doorknob and leave the dog there for a timeout. Do not do this in anger—remember you are training, not seeking retribution. The dog will probably whine and cry. Wait for a lull before letting the dog rejoin the family (otherwise you will be rewarding the dog for whining). You want the dog to realize that biting immediately puts a stop to all the fun and settling down quietly lets a dog have another chance.

BRINGING KIDS AND DOGS TOGETHER

There's no doubt that bringing a dog into the family adds more chores and another kind of necessary supervision. But researchers have also found that families with pets tend to be happier. Dogs always stand ready to give love and attention to each family member, and they provide a great topic of conversation. In fact, even outside the family, telling a story about a pet is an almost instant way to get conversation flowing. People who might not ordinarily speak to each other will eagerly tell the latest exploits of their dog or cat to any and all concerned.

When Is a Child Ready for a Dog?

If there isn't already a dog in your home, part of keeping everyone safe and secure comes from knowing when to add one. Though preschoolers may beg for a dog with great fervor, this age group generally makes for inappropriate dog companions. Children this young have very erratic movements. They may injure small pets by dropping them or manhandling them, inviting retaliation. They are just learning to control their movements, and their actions can be sudden and unpredictable. It's better to ignore the pleading or offer the child the chance to prove that he or she can be responsible with a less demanding pet such as a fish or a bird.

Early school-age children, say 6 to 10 years of age, should be ready to be responsible around a dog, and maybe even to perform some of the duties related to having one. Though too young to walk the dog alone, they can help with feeding, pooper scooping and exercising the dog with games (see the last section of this chapter for suggestions). If possible, children should attend a training class to help start them on the right path to communicating with canines, but a large part of that responsibility is yours. If a child sees you losing your temper with the dog, you are sending the message that this is how to deal with problems.

Children older than 10 should be capable of behaving well around dogs, and even of providing most of the dog's care. Some might even be able to walk the dog, depending on the child's and animal's size and temperament. Several trainers and behaviorists have suggested that a child becomes responsible enough to interact well with a dog at 10 years. However, parents should be aware of their particular child's level of maturity. Some 8-year-olds are remarkably conscious of and responsible for their actions, while some 12-year-olds still don't seem to have grasped the concept. Early and ongoing training in respect for all forms of life is essential. Enough evidence has been accumulated to show that cruelty toward animals in childhood often develops into extreme antisocial behavior in adults.

One caution to keep in mind: Many books and trainers will advise that you must structure the home "pack" so that all humans rank above the dog, but this flies in the face of canine social structure. Dogs are expert at interpreting events and interactions and understand that children are just that—children. And children (puppies, if you will) simply don't rank above adults in the pack structure. Adult dogs will show great forbearance toward puppies and see that they stay safe from harm, but they won't consider them pack leaders. It's futile to try to convince them otherwise. That doesn't mean that children can't train dogs themselves or handle them in competition. It just means the dog sees a child differently than she sees an adult.

Choosing a Breed or Mix of Breeds

The AKC now recognizes about 150 breeds of dogs, and about 400 breeds are acknowledged worldwide. Then, of course, there are the mixed breeds, combining two, three or a dozen of these breeds in a nearly infinite variety. How do you begin to choose? The answers to some basic questions will help you to pare down the possibilities.

- What age are the children in the home?

  Preschoolers and many children younger than 10 are not good candidates for toy breeds or young puppies. Older dogs of larger breeds will be safer for everyone. Don't think that dogs more than eight weeks old will not bond with your family. The vast majority of dogs will transfer their love and loyalty to a new family quite readily. In fact, older puppies—around five months of age—are easier to house-train (having a greater attention span and better control of their bladders) and to train in general.

- How much daily exercise will the dog receive?

  Be honest about this. Don't make a dog a part of your New Year's resolution to get out and exercise more. We all know that we aren't very resolute about our resolutions, and if you choose a breed such as a Brittany or Australian Shepherd who needs a good deal of exercise and then don't follow through, you will be creating problems. Tiny toys can be exercised effectively indoors, even if they are high-energy.

- Can you afford the dog you choose?

  While any dog can quickly become a significant expense should a health emergency arise, larger dogs do cost more to maintain in general. Flea preventives, doses of medication, food servings and even collars and crates are larger and thus more expensive. Some breeds are more susceptible to genetic health problems, which can certainly add up costs in a hurry.

- Are you an experienced dog owner or a first-timer?

  Some breeds are definitely more of a challenge to the novice dog owner. Trainers are seeing lots of Jack Russell Terriers in class with owners who are desperate to get control of their dogs. If you are looking for your first dog, it's probably better to stay away from what some call the "hard" breeds.

- Are you willing to groom a dog, or take her to a groomer regularly?

Coated breeds do need more maintenance than their wash-and-wear cousins. You may love the look of a Shetland Sheepdog or Cocker Spaniel, but the dog doesn't stay looking that way on her own. At a minimum, a canine coat requires weekly brushing to prevent matting. If you plan on using a dog groomer, be sure to factor that cost into your dog-related expenses.

- Are you house-proud?

  Puppies have accidents. Dogs shed and come in the house with muddy feet. Tails or boisterous bodies can sweep possessions to the floor. If all this sounds horrific to you, you're probably better off having a hamster or, at most, a cat.

- Do you live in the city, suburbs or country?

  While you can live in an urban apartment and keep a Border Collie exercised and entertained, it takes considerably more effort on your part than if you lived on acreage out in the country (preferably with a flock of sheep). Some dogs fit into city life better, and they aren't always the breeds you'd expect. For example, Greyhounds are great couch potatoes, content to curl up by the fire.

- What climate do you live in?

  Sleek short-coated breeds without a lot of body fat such as Whippets and Greyhounds and many of the toy breeds chill easily and are reluctant to venture outdoors on wintry days. This can complicate housetraining and exercise. Coated breeds may relish the cold and snow, but literally melt all over your house as ice balls attached to their hair thaw out. Heavily coated breeds such as Alaskan Malamutes and Keeshonden may suffer in hot climes. Make it easier on yourself and choose a dog that fits the weather where you live.

- What's the temperament?

  Of course, when bringing dogs and children together, the dog's temperament is of utmost importance. Some books will indicate whether a breed is "good with children" or "unsuitable for children." Although these are generalities, it's probably wise to avoid breeds indicated as "unsuitable." Choosing a breed said to be "good with children" doesn't guarantee smooth sailing. You still need to assess, train and supervise.

- Male or female?

  You may hear a number of claims regarding canine gender, such as the idea that females are easier to train or males are more aggressive. I haven't found any of them to be true. The main gender-related differences are that males will be more intent on marking their territory, making walks more of a challenge (though they can be trained not to do this). Females will cost more to have spayed and may have a greater tendency to problems with incontinence when they are old. Unspayed females will certainly come into heat, creating both a mess and the nuisance of visiting male suitors. Unaltered males will have more of a tendency to roam. Other than that, behavioral traits have more to do with individuals than with gender.

- Mixed breed or purebred?

  I don't deny it: I'm a fan of mixed breeds. Mixing breeds can tone down some of a breed's strong characteristics—a Border Collie mixed with Labrador, for example, may be less hyperactive.

Where to Find Your Dog

Most sources will tell you to buy your dog from a reputable breeder, and that's certainly a good option. Before exploring what constitutes a "good" breeder and how you find one, however, I'd like to explore some other avenues.

Some dogs in shelters are there due to "behavior problems," but many others end up in these circumstances because their owners have died or their owners have failed in their responsibility in some way. These are well-behaved pets who have found themselves abandoned through no fault of their own. Some are mixed breeds, some are purebreds. Some may have only a few years left themselves, while some are young dogs with their lives still ahead of them. They are likely to be housetrained and often obedience trained, so they can make your life much simpler.

If you do not have a lot of experience with dogs, how do you find these gems? Shelters are much better at providing information than they used to be. Though there are still places where nearly all dogs are listed as Poodle mix, Lab cross, German Shepherd mix, hound or Pit Bull, and where dogs are placed into pens and largely ignored, more shelters have volunteer dog walkers and employ adoption counselors who can evaluate each dog's potential and can assist you in making a good choice.

If you can't set foot in a shelter, or you know you will be swayed by the first pretty face you see, then rescue groups are a good way to go. These groups have breed coordinators who go into shelters looking for any dogs of a particular breed. Many will also include mixes that probably do contain their chosen breed. You can find national breed rescue coordinators through the AKC web site, and you can view dogs needing homes at petfinders.com and other similar web sites. Seattle Purebred Dog Rescue has prospective adopters fill out questionnaires detailing the home the dog will be going to. They will try to match up the breed or mix of the breed requested, and will tell adopters if they feel the breed is unsuitable for the home. They will also evaluate the dog they are considering, and one of their members will accompany the dog to meet the family. Other groups around the country have similar programs.

You can do all the same things with a rescue that you can with a pedigreed dog from a breeder, with the single exception of conformation (the dog show, the beauty pageant of the canine world). Pedigree confers nothing on a dog other than acceptance by a kennel club. It's not any guarantee of health, temperament or long life.

If you decide to buy from a breeder, you still have to do your homework. All breeders are not created equal, and puppies from those who are irresponsible or uneducated are likely to come with both health and temperament problems. Get recommendations on breeders from your veterinarian, local dog club and the AKC or UKC. You may be surprised to learn that the nearest breeder is a hundred miles away or more (especially if you have settled on a less common breed) and that the waiting list for puppies is long. Or you may see classified ads every day and have a dozen breeders in your hometown for the breed you're attracted to. I suggest that you ignore the newspaper ads. Responsible breeders have more potential homes than they have puppies.

Start calling the breeders on your list. Ask how their adult dogs used for breeding get along with children, and how their puppies are socialized to children. Letting puppies know what children are and how to deal with them is very important. Expect to be asked extensive questions about your family and home. If a breeder doesn't question you either on the phone or during a visit, then either you've failed some sort of criteria without even knowing it and the breeder isn't going to sell you one of her dogs, or this is not a responsible breeder and you shouldn't obtain your dog here. Move along to the next name on your list.

Don't be in a hurry. Once your family has decided to add a dog, it may suddenly seem an urgent matter, but this is a long-term commitment and must be taken seriously.

What to Look for in a Family Dog

If you have reliable advisors to help you, you should certainly listen to what they say, but you can also make some assessments of your own. If you are visiting a litter of puppies, crouch down a little distance from them. Ignore any puppies who hang back and don't come to you at all. Also ignore any puppies who leap on you, chew on your hands and try to keep the other puppies from reaching you. It's not that these are necessarily bad dogs, but they are less likely to fit in easily with children. What you're looking for is a pup who comes up to you in a secure, forthright manner but doesn't frantically vie for your attention.

Pick up any puppy you are considering and cradle her in your arms, lying on her back. Smile and be relaxed, but don't interact more than that. Expect some initial struggling, but the puppy should settle after a few moments and lie happily in your arms. If a pup doesn't struggle at all, check that she's not just so frightened that she's rigid—you don't want that either.

When all the puppies are on the ground, make a sudden loud noise and watch their reactions. Startling, jumping or running a few steps away are all acceptable as long as the pup then recovers and comes to investigate. No reaction at all could mean that the pup is insensitive to noise (good) or deaf (bad). To be sure, you'll need to check further into the pup's hearing.

Next, do something mildly annoying and slightly painful to a puppy. Pinch the base of an ear or the skin between the toes. You want a puppy who whines or tries to pull away, but then relaxes when you stop. Puppies who scream as if they're being killed or who try to bite you to get you to cease and desist are probably touch-sensitive and not good choices for homes with children. These little tests, combined with information from your advisors, should result in a good choice and a pup who will fit well into your household.

An adult dog may be a little slower to warm to you, but should be cordial toward visitors in her home environment. A dog that has already lived with children will likely be successful with your family as well, provided your children understand how to behave around dogs.

If you're looking at adults in a shelter, keep in mind that dogs caged amid dozens of other dogs will probably not be exhibiting their true personalities. Watch for dogs who come to the front of the pen to greet you. They may be barking with excitement (though they should stop after you've passed) or silent and somber (dogs often suffer from depression in shelters, especially if they have been taken from a household). Remember these dogs and ask to take any that appeal to you, one at a time, to whatever space the shelter has available for prospective adopters to get to know the dogs. In these quieter surroundings, more of the dog's true personality may become apparent.

DEVELOPING FUN AND SAFE GAMES FOR KIDS AND DOGS

Kids and dogs are natural companions. Both really know how to have a good time and enjoy life to the fullest. With a few basic safety procedures imposed by adults and enforced by everyone, their interaction can be wonderful thing.

One of the best games for everyone to play is hide-and-seek. The dog is always "it," and doesn't seem to mind at all. It takes a little while to teach everyone how to play this game, but it's well worth the time.

Start by holding the dog while the child leaves the room saying, "Come find me, Ranger." The child hides somewhere easy to find, just out of sight. Release the dog while telling her "Go find Jenny." If the dog isn't immediately successful, have the child call her from the hiding place. When the find is made, praise the dog excitedly and give her a treat. As the dog gets the idea, make the hiding places more difficult, then don't let the dog watch the child go out of sight. You can also take the game outdoors, to expand the territory.

By teaching the dog to find different people—use each person's name as you send the dog to find him or her—you can have everyone but the dog handler hide. The handler sends the dog to find one person. That person then rewards the dog and sends her on to find the next person. This game is fun for the kids (and the adults, truth be told) and gives the dog a great chance to use her nose and her brain. When it's raining or freezing outside and everyone is restless and bored, you can play hide-and-seek and entertain the entire household.

Fetch is another great game and burns up even more of the dog's energy. It also requires some basic training. The retriever types will be naturally eager to fetch, but they need to understand that they must not grab at a ball or other object being held by a human, and that they should give or drop the object once they have retrieved it. Dogs who are not retrievers can be taught to retrieve with clicker training (or through Sue Sternberg's inducive method—her small book on the subject is listed in the Resources appendix).

Chapter 11, Solutions to Common Problems, explains the "give/drop" procedure. To help enforce this important concept, it's best to have two fetch objects. When the dog brings back one fetch, show the second object as you command "drop" or "give," and when the dog complies, throw the second object. You can then pick up the first (probably now slimy) object while the dog is fetching the second.

There are several devices available that allow you to pick up a tennis ball without having to bend over or handle it and help you to throw it farther. Kids may find these items make fetch more fun.

Teaching tricks can be a great experience for kids and lots more fun than obedience training. It's important to supervise younger children during any training efforts. Depending on the dog's temperament and the child's maturity, 12-year-olds may be ready to do some training on their own.

Some tricks that are generally easy to teach and fun to show off are wave, roll over, play dead and jump through a hoop. Having the child practice commands with the dog will help to ensure that they understand each other. If the child can also use a few basic commands such as "sit," "down" and "stay," he'll have a positive way to direct the dog's behavior and can avoid injuries caused by dogs jumping up on small people.

We've talked about playing tug before. It's a good, safe game, even for older children, as long as all the rules are followed. In this instance, the children might be harder to control than the dog. Children have to understand the need to retain control. Playing tug can't be just a 20-minute free-for-all. The game must stop frequently with a "give" command, a brief timeout, then an invitation to "tug" again. If the dog doesn't respond to the "give" command, an adult must step in to enforce the rules and end the game. Any contact between dog teeth and human flesh, even if accidental, means an immediate end to the game.

Another game you may remember from early childhood is also fun to play with the dog as a participant. In traditional red light/ green light, children hurry toward the opposite end of the course when the person who is "it" has his back turned. When "it" says "red light" and turns around, everyone must freeze in place. Anyone caught moving is out. The first one to reach the person at the end of the course wins the game. In the canine version, contestants and dogs cross the course together. The handlers must have their dogs heel when moving. When the handlers stop, the dogs must sit. They must stay sitting until "it" gives the "green light" signal and handlers start moving forward again.

Kids and dogs playing games together will burn off some of the abundant energy both have, and will help to cement their relationship with one another.

X-tra Sensory

Do animal communicators really communicate?
Do dogs have souls?

> I have sometimes thought of the final cause of dogs having
> such short lives, and I am quite satisfied it is in compassion
> to the human race; for if we suffer so much in losing a dog
> after an acquaintance of 10 or 12 years, what would it be if
> they were to live double that time?
>
> Sir Walter Scott

Within the Winnebago tribe there is a clan called the Hotcâk, *which means*
Dog Clan or Wolf Clan. (The Winnebago make no hard distinction between
wolves and dogs—their word for dog is cûk *and wolf is* cûktcâk, *or "great*
dog.") The closeness of dogs and humans is reflected in the social status of their
dogs. Dogs are often treated with great affection and have the status of members
of the family circle. At dinner, a place is set out for the dog in the family dining
area. The sounds dogs make when they try to communicate with humans are
understood as a form of language. There are members of the clan, called
cûkhit'enakuns, who have learned the language of dogs. These cûkhit'enakuns
are often called upon to discover what dogs are trying to communicate.

Can we actually communicate mind-to-mind with our dogs? It's a
question sure to raise hackles on both sides of the issue. But even if
you think telepathy is just a lot of New Age nonsense, your thoughts
and attitude *do* matter in your dealings with your dog. The dog is a
creature with a highly developed ability to read body language and, as

187

any good criminologist will attest, your thoughts and feelings are reflected in the signals your body sends.

THE MIND-BODY CONNECTION

Those who interrogate people for a living have no doubts about the mind-body connection. Read up on the subject and you learn that people look up and to the left while trying to recall some fact, blink more rapidly when nervous and exhibit all sorts of behavior associated with their mental state. The "lie detector" mechanism reads increased blood pressure, breathing rate and skin temperature associated with the stress of lying (which is why people who don't find lying stressful can "beat" the machine.)

So what does this mind-body connection mean when it comes to communicating with your dog? It means that your dog is more likely to understand the message sent by your body than the message you try to send with your words. If, for example, you are about to perform your first freestyle routine in public and you are breathing fast and shallow with your hands all over the dog, or you're pacing and fidgeting, then telling the dog, "It's OK, just relax," this is going to have about as much effect as spitting on a bonfire. Your body is communicating to the dog that you're nervous, worried and uptight. She will likely decide there must be some good reason for this reaction and go on high alert, too.

I've had many handlers from a wide variety of sports tell me, "My dog is perfect in practice, but messes up when we get in the ring. What can I do?" Or, "Why doesn't my dog have the same attitude when we compete as when we practice?" If this is your experience, it's likely because *you* are different in the ring, and so your dog is different in response. Your body language has changed; you probably even smell different.

My first competition dog, Serling, taught me the value of focusing on the important things in life (which do not include blue ribbons and trophies) and learning to relax. We earned our CD (Companion Dog) title with me as the typical uptight handler. We even got our first leg toward our CDX (Companion Dog Excellent), the second level of obedience. But as we competed, Serling became more and more the clown. He threw tricks into the middle of

Relaxed body posture = relaxed mind.

obedience routines. He left heel position to run "puppy sprints" around the ring, and when handlers went out of sight for the three-minute sit, he came and "found" me.

Spectators found my dog highly amusing and, finally, so did I. As I learned to let go and laugh at his antics and started going into the ring with an easy attitude of "can't wait to see what he'll pull this time," we started not just qualifying, but winning, including a High in Trial at the Cow Palace in San Francisco. It finally dawned on me that Serling was doing his best to put me at ease, and he was actually quite good at it. My walls are full of ribbons, and trophies line my shelves thanks to that dog, but there could be nothing more important

Try It Yourself

If you've never practiced meditation or visualization, you'll need some practice.

There are a lot of ways to go about it. One that seems to work well for a lot of people is counting backward. Sit in a quiet room and try to relax. Picture the number 100 in your head, then picture pushing it away from you down a tunnel until it's out of sight. Do the same with 99, then 98 and so on. When you're handling the numbers well and have managed to dismiss most of the other thousands of thoughts normally floating around in your head, create your visualization picture. See yourself winning some doggie event, or just picture your dog not barking at the delivery person, if that's your concern. Hold onto that visualization as long as you can. When other thoughts start to seep back in, you're done.

Another method works more on relaxation than concentration. This one is better done lying down. Start by relaxing the muscles in your feet, silently telling yourself something like, "My toes are relaxing. My feet are relaxed and I can feel them sinking into the bed." Then move on to the ankles, the shins, the knees, working your way up your body, relaxing each set of muscles in turn. By the time you get to your neck, your body should feel very light and your mind will be open to all sorts of things. Both of these methods are used by insomniacs to help their brains gear down so they can go to sleep.

A third method is simply to sit quietly with your eyes closed, and as you exhale each breath, say the word "calm" in your head. When random thoughts pop into your head, just push them away and repeat "calm." Different methods work better for different people. If you want to explore this further, there are plenty of books, videotapes, even classes on meditation and relaxation.

than the lesson he taught me: We're here to have fun, so just relax and enjoy it.

We are a very competitive species. We invest an awful lot in winning—just look at the parents at a Little League game—and we really hate to lose. But what's *really* important in the whole scheme of things? Is your dog going to love you less if the ribbon isn't blue, or if you don't have one at all? Of course not. The only thing the dog's worried about is your mental state. The more you can relax, breathe deep, move loosely and communicate that all is right with the world, the better you'll be, the better your dog will be and the more you'll both enjoy whatever it is you're doing.

This is also, I think, the reason behind visualization. Handlers are often advised to picture their dog doing the perfect retrieve, having a flawless agility run or stacking and gaiting beautifully in the conformation ring. While some coaches may actually believe that the image is being mentally projected to the dog, most are simply trying to instill confidence in the handler so she may be calmer and more capable of that good performance. In Novice obedience, where you have to stand across the ring from the line of dogs performing the one-minute sit, I often used to close my eyes so that I could visualize my dog sitting straight and tall rather than watch him play games. (Do you have any idea what it's like to see your 80-pound dog sit up and beg for half the allotted time? Technically, he was still sitting.) But I hadn't really gotten the idea yet. I was visualizing out of desperation, not in hopes of relaxation.

CONNECTING MENTALLY WITH YOUR DOG

While I am heartily skeptical of a whole lot of claims that "animal communicators" make, I do believe in the possibility of mental communication with dogs. It's hard, after all, to disbelieve in something you're fairly sure you've experienced yourself. Yes, you read that right— I think I've experienced direct mental communication with an animal. Scoff if you must, but if you do, you may as well skip over this section—you've already decided and you won't get anything out of it.

The idea of parapsychology and mental telepathy has always been intellectually attractive because scientists keep telling us that we only use 10 or 15 percent of our brain. The rest of it must be there for some reason. Maybe it can do all those wondrous things that idiot savants can do, like immense mathematical calculations or playing any piece of music they've ever heard. Maybe it can link to another brain and send and receive.

I do know that some people "have a way" with animals. Treacherous horses never kick or act up with them, aggressive dogs don't growl or bite and even wild animals approach them. My father is one of these people. I think my dad, and others like him, just act instinctively around animals, without any idea that they may be communicating on a whole other level.

Animal communicators insist that we all have this ability. They may be right, but I think for a lot of people it's buried so deeply that it's inaccessible. Many people maintain that children routinely have and use this ability, until they are taught that they can't talk with the dog or the cat, and that they're just imagining things. Eventually they leave the idea of communication behind in childhood. So before you dismiss the subject entirely, think back—did you have childhood conversations with a pet?

When people try this with their own dogs, they have practically no way to know if they're actually communicating or not. The most frequent comment when people try this is "I feel like I'm making it up." Animal communicator Lauren McCall suggests working with someone else's dog so that you can receive validation from her owner. "You really need to get verification from others about animals that are not your own," McCall says. "Otherwise, you never know if it's your imagination or a genuine connection." She notes that most people go through the "crazy person syndrome" where they think they are just having conversations with themselves. But repeated examples of validation can pull you past that phase. Maybe you can find a friend who would like to try it, too, so you can validate each other.

First, you have to find the best way to quiet your mind (see the box on page 190). If you've ever done meditation, that's a good way to start. A favorite yoga routine may help. Anything you can do to clear your mind and put yourself in a neutral state is good.

You Can Quote Me

If you are comfortable with emotions, you may find yourself sensing what an animal is feeling. Visual people get pictures or images. Those of us who are verbal and like to use words tend to get communications with words and sentences. Most of us get a combination of things.

Lauren McCall, animal communicator

Sit quietly with your dog(s) and see what happens.

McCall leads guided meditation in her classes, not only to help students achieve that neutral state, but also to help them resist the temptation to filter any messages they may receive. Communication may come in whatever manner is most comfortable for the receiver, whether that's words, images or emotions.

Practice at home first, so you're comfortable with whatever relaxation/meditation methods you'll be using, then go to your friend's home. Sit quietly in a room with the friend's dog. Do your relaxation routine and see what happens. You can form the thought "I would like to communicate" or you can just try to open your mind and wait. Don't give up too soon—try to maintain the relaxed open state for 15 minutes or so. When you're ready to stop, tell your friend any impressions that floated into your mind. See if anything makes a connection with your friend.

An entire roomful of people was doing this exercise at a dog trainers' conference, attempting to tune in to the Bernese Mountain Dog at the front of the room. I received a very strong picture of running and leaping, with everything a blur to either side, then smashing headfirst into a vertical surface. This made no sense, but I dutifully reported it, and a person on the other side of the room immediately said, "Oh, that must have been Doogie." Her dog, Doogie, had come in straight from doing a flyball demonstration, where the dog races over four low hurdles, grabs a tennis ball from a spring-loaded wooden box and races back. I didn't even know he was in the room. But he sure enjoyed flyball, and I got a dog's-eye view of what the sport is like. The point is, don't throw away anything, no matter how silly it seems. You might be tuning in to the cat or the parrot in the next room instead of the dog.

Return the favor and invite your friend to come to your house and try it with your dog. Who knows? Maybe you'll learn something.

Often, it's hard for people to get started communicating with their animals. McCall instructs her students to mentally frame a question with a concrete answer, such as "What's your favorite food?" or "Do you have a toy that you like?" If no answer seems to be coming, she advises imagining one yourself. You may be blocking the response, and in "making up" an answer, you are actually letting the communication through without realizing it. After asking a couple of questions and making up the answers, many people find that they begin to receive more definite communication.

When you are beginning, it may also help to be in physical contact with the animal. McCall remembers that touching the dog seemed to work as an amplifier when she was beginning. As she

I had Nestle's hips x-rayed within months of adopting him, even though he never limped, because I "knew" something was wrong. The X rays showed very bad joints, which we are managing.

I never communicate harder than when introducing a new pup into the pack, telling everyone they're all still loved and to please get along.

became more accomplished, she could work with the animal nearby without actually touching her; then it became fine if the animal wandered in and out. Help yourself during your early attempts by sitting with a hand on the dog or leaning against each other.

I'm convinced that being at least open to the idea that my dogs can communicate with me has enabled me to catch health problems much earlier than would otherwise be possible. Even if it just makes me more perceptive in observing my dogs and there really isn't any mind-to-mind connection going on, the effect is the same and can be tremendously valuable.

Don't forget that communication works both ways. If your dog can communicate with you, then you should be able to use the same pathways. The procedure is much the same. The counting backward technique works well because it involves forming images in your mind. When you are concentrating well on the numbers, form the picture you want to send. Want the dog to stop pulling on the leash? Send a picture of you and your dog walking, with a nice loose loop of lead between you. Is barking a problem? Picture the dog sitting and watching attentively but quietly while the UPS truck and driver come and go. I'm not saying this will solve all of your problems, but it might help your dog realize what you want. You still have to make it worth the dog's while to stop pulling or stop barking.

Lauren McCall provided a recent communication she had with a dog so you can get some idea of how things might go. She communicates largely in words; others might see pictures instead. The dog is Gaston. The family is a couple with a young child. They had recently lost another dog, Bella.

Lauren: How did you feel about living in New York?

Gaston: It's OK. Better here though. I like this place here better. It's not so hot and not so cold. I like that.

Lauren: Are you happy and content with us?

Gaston: I love you and you are my family. It took me a while to get used to the little one. But I love him now too and I will help you take care of him.

Lauren: Do you like this house, this area?

Gaston: Yes, but the slippery floors are not my favorite. The area is quiet, I like that. I don't like too much noise: it makes me nervous after awhile.

Lauren: How would you feel about having another dog in the house? We would like to think about giving an older dog that needs a family a home.

Gaston: I'm not sure. Things are OK now.

Lauren: We thought you might like a companion.

Gaston: No, I have you and the little one. It's enough for me. Too much change. We move, Bella dies, we move. It's enough. Time to rest and just be.

DO DOGS HAVE SOULS?

The word "animal" derives from the Latin *anima*, which means soul, so I would venture that our ancestors believed animals have souls. This idea was buried under scientific scorn by Aristotle, then Thomas Aquinas, and especially by René Descartes with his concept of animals as mere clockwork machines. This was a viewpoint that made it convenient to excuse vivisection and the general mistreatment of animals, but the tide turned as people came to view animals as valued companions.

When people quote the Bible to support their position that animals do not have souls, they ignore the fact that the Bible has been translated many times, into and out of many languages. Scholars who can read the Bible in versions closer to the original point out that translations often reflect the thinking of the era in which they were

How could anyone say this is just an animated machine with no feelings?

You Can Quote Me

You think dogs will not be in heaven? I tell you, they will be there long before any of us.

Robert Louis Stevenson, poet, novelist and essayist

translated. Thus, the same phrase has been translated as "living soul" in reference to humans and "living creature" in reference to animals.

Today, "official" church positions, particularly in the Judeo-Christian tradition, often differ diametrically from the opinions of individual clergy and practitioners. In private conversations with representatives of many faiths, I found that most of the major Christian denominations believe that animals have souls. Some Catholics believe pets would be in heaven, if only for our sake (it wouldn't be heaven without our pets), but others give them full soul-endowed status. Mormon teaching holds that every living thing is spiritual and will be present in the afterlife. In Judaism, a *tzadick*, or person who is spiritually evolved, is connected to "the soul of his animal." The idea that everything is endowed with a spirit and every spirit returns to the Creator runs throughout Jewish teaching. In fact, Judaism has a mandate (*tsa'ar ba'alei hayim*) to prevent the "sorrow of living creatures"— all living creatures.

Other religions are more explicit in their acceptance of the spirit of animals. Muslim scripture teaches the equality of animals, including ideas such as "All creatures are like a family to God" and "He has assigned the earth to all living creatures." A good deed done for an animal earns as much respect as one done for a human, while a cruelty to one is as bad as a cruelty to the other.

Both Buddhism and Hinduism, with their belief in reincarnation, necessarily believe that all animals have souls. A human can be reborn in the form of a dog, so the dog must have a soul or the equation doesn't work. Also, the soul returns in a specific form for some reason, to learn a particular lesson or perform some deed, so harming or killing an animal may stop that soul from completing the task necessary to raise it to a higher plane of consciousness. And that is a grievous harm indeed. The very first of the Five Precepts of Buddhist teaching (the foundation of the religion's view of ethical conduct) is simply not to harm any sentient beings.

Jainism, one of the religions of India, provides a strict code of conduct in regard to other living beings. Followers of Jainism are not only vegans, but they also cover their faces with masks to avoid inhaling tiny insects.

CHAPTER 11

Solutions to Common Problems

How can you use communication to resolve problem behavior?
When is compromise the right solution?

> To a man, the greatest blessing is individual liberty; to a dog
> it is the last word in despair.
>
> William Lyon Phelps,
> author and Yale University professor

*There was once a mighty king who oppressed his subjects, and was therefore
much hated by them. Yet even this king desired to see the Tathagata (enlightened
one) when he came into the kingdom. When the king arrived at the resting place
of the Tathagata, he asked, "Can you tell this king a lesson to divert his mind
and benefit him at the same time?"*

The Tathagata replied, "I shall tell the parable of the hungry dog."

*"There was a wicked tyrant in the kingdom, and the god Indra came down
to earth in the shape of a hunter, bringing with him the demon Matali in the
form of a dog of truly enormous size. Hunter and dog entered the palace, where
the dog began to howl with such vigor that the royal buildings shook to their
foundations. The tyrant had the hunter brought before him and asked why the
dog howled so. The hunter replied, "The dog is hungry." So the frightened king
ordered food prepared for the animal. But everything from the royal banquet
disappeared down the dog's throat, and still the dog howled. Food was prepared
until the royal storehouses stood nearly empty, but still the dog howled on. The
desperate king asked, "Will nothing satisfy the cravings of that beast?" "Nothing,"
replied the hunter, "Except perhaps the flesh of his enemies." "Who are his enemies?" asked the tyrant eagerly. The hunter replied, "The dog will howl as long*

as there are people going hungry in the kingdom, for his enemies are any who practice injustice and oppress the poor." The tyrant, who was truly an oppressor of the poor, paled and trembled, and for the first time in his life began to listen to the teachings of righteousness."

The king to whom the Tathagata had related the parable was also pale and trembling. The Blessed One told him, "The Tathagata can quicken the spiritual ears of the powerful, and when thou, great king, hears the dog bark, think of the teachings of the Buddha, and thou may yet learn to pacify the monster."

You've been reading about communication with your dog for 10 chapters now. Have you put any of what you've learned into practice, or are you confused by it all and more unsure than ever how to deal with your dog? In this chapter, we'll get more hands-on and I'll explain how everything we've been talking about comes into play when you're training your dog or trying to address any behavior problems you may be confronting.

When working on communication, behavior and problem solving, you've got to be realistic. You've got a terrier who digs? No kidding! It's what they were made for. If you understand this, you can work toward a compromise that will suit both you and your pet, rather than resort to punitive measures that will frustrate you, may make the dog neurotic and probably won't work.

Is barking a problem? There are half a dozen or more different triggers for barking, and addressing the wrong one won't solve your

---

 You Can Quote Me

I try to get people to think about the animal's needs and letting them have a variety of choices. Sometimes they have unrealistic expectations. For example, they take a two-year-old dog out to let it pee and they want to bring it right back in the house without letting it sniff or exercise or socialize with any other dogs or explore the world or watch the air or whatever it is the dog wants to do. So the dog takes longer and longer to pee every day. There's a situation where the person is not meeting the dog's needs.

Karen Overall, veterinarian, columnist and animal behaviorist problem. Some dogs just aren't cut out to lounge at home all day, content with a walk before you leave for work and after you get home. You could use some environmental enrichment to occupy the dog and might have to hire a pet walker or enroll your canine in doggy day care.

Some "problems" aren't things the dog can do anything about. Dogs can't help it that their urine burns grass and causes yellow spots. If it bothers you, it's your job to give your dog an alternate place to do her business and take the time to train her to use it. Dogs accommodate our rules all the time. You can be a little understanding and bend a little, too.

SOLUTIONS TO SOME COMMON PROBLEMS

Some of the rifts between humans and dogs result directly from behavior that is natural to the dog. Barking is normal canine behavior. So are digging, chewing and running around like a maniac. However, owners often see these activities as behaviors to be eradicated. Because some of these behaviors—chewing in particular—are expressions of nervousness, attempts to get rid of them can often result in even worse problems. Nervous dogs who are punished for chewing the chair leg while the humans are away get even more nervous about being left home alone as a result.

Dogs use their mouths to explore their world and to release tension, bark to point out items of interest and dig to reach cool dirt to lie in or because their heritage tells them to. Once you acknowledge that these are nothing more than natural behaviors, you can work out a compromise with your dog.

Compromises are not all that difficult. In the last few years, new products designed to hold treats in ways that encourage dogs to work to get at them have gained popularity and kept home-alone dogs happy for hours. They can even entertain the dog while you are home and need to devote your attention to other things. Some dogs who particularly delight in chewing branches have owners understanding enough to provide opportunities for them to indulge in this activity, whether in the yard or in an easily cleanable area such as a laundry room. Worries that the dog will see this as license to chew everything are almost entirely unfounded.

Barking dogs can be taught to speak on cue and then also learn to be quiet on cue. Digging dogs—especially terriers and Dachshunds—can have their own selected location where digging is not only legal, but encouraged.

Digging

Let's start with the digging dog. Plenty of people find this behavior a problem. Some of the reasons dogs dig are to

- Escape the yard
- Make a cool pit to lie in
- Hunt underground prey, real or imagined (those terriers!)
- Bury or dig up food treats or toys
- Occupy themselves and burn off excess energy

With the exception of escaping the yard, which we'll get to in a minute, these all have the same solution: Give the dog an acceptable place to dig and train her to use it—just as we give human children sandboxes to play in.

The two major objections to this idea concern aesthetics and training time. You can design it to fit in with whatever décor suits you and your yard, or you can put potted plants around the outside. Rather than be negative, look at this as an opportunity to include a new design element in your yard, one that is likely to engender some lively conversation ("It's a sandbox for your dog?!"). The pit only has to be longer than your dog and can be a little less wide. Leave a small low section on one side for a doorway and make the sides a couple of feet higher than the level of the sand and loose dirt filling the box to help keep the contents contained. You can dig the pit down into the ground if you prefer a lower profile. Fill the box with a mix of sand and dirt. If you think your dog is digging to reach cool earth, place the box in the shade. As to the training, yes, it will take some time, but so will repeatedly filling in holes and replanting dislodged flowers or bushes. And you're much more likely to keep your temper with the training than with the yard renovation. It may not even take very long. My latest dog, Nestle, required only two sandbox play sessions of about 10 minutes each, followed by a couple of days of observation and occasional redirection.

To train your dog to use the sandbox, bury some hard treats (biscuits, for example) and a toy or two in the sand. Bring your dog over to the box, encourage her to get in and excitedly dig up one of the treats or toys and give it to the dog. Start digging a little bit in another place and encourage her to join in. If you've already spent weeks or months yelling at your dog for digging, it will take longer to get the idea across that this is a place where digging is acceptable. Repeat the visit to the sandbox and the digging up treats routine a few times a day until the dog seems to be getting the idea. *Don't* drag the dog to the sandbox. This experience should be fun and upbeat. If the dog visits the box on her own, smile and praise her.

For the next few days, try to keep an eye on your dog when she's outside. If she starts to dig anywhere but in the box, get the dog's attention and say "dig in your box" (or whatever you choose) while encouraging the dog to the sandbox. Praise her to the heavens if she gets in and starts digging.

The communication here is very simple. The dog is saying, "I want to dig." You're saying, "OK, I'm giving you this great place to dig—use it and we'll both be happy." It's a win-win situation.

The dog who digs to escape the yard is an entirely different issue, and a digging pit will not solve the problem. This dog either finds home just too boring and is escaping to find entertainment, is responding to the allure of the mating game (both males and females are known to be seized by wanderlust in their search for "romance") or simply has to constantly see what's over the next hill (Siberian Huskies are known for this). For full-bore escape artists, you'll have to manage the situation by keeping the dog indoors or in a concrete-floor dog run when no one's around to supervise. For the dog who's merely bored, you can help resolve the problem with a program of environmental enrichment, which we'll explore later in this chapter.

Jumping Up

A lot of people advocate teaching the dog to sit on command, then using the command to tell the dog to sit rather than jump up. That can work, but I prefer the method demonstrated by Terry Ryan to dog-trainers-in-training, using shelter dogs as subjects. Here's is how it works: Someone holds the dog on leash. This person does not interact with the dog, but just stands there like a post. Holding some yummy treats, you approach the dog and act very friendly. If the dog tries to jump when you are almost within range, say "too bad," turn around and walk away. Wait a few seconds and try again.

Every time the dog reacts by pulling or jumping or leaping around, you turn and walk away. You don't yell at the dog, and the person holding the leash doesn't yank on the dog. There's no emotion involved. The dog is not giving the response you want, so you simply reject it.

Sooner or later—nearly always in the first half dozen tries—the dog will realize what she's doing isn't working and will try something else. Sitting usually appears pretty quickly once the dog decides to experiment. As soon as the dog sits when you approach, continue forward quickly and give the dog the treat, trying to reward the dog while she is still sitting.

Move away and approach your dog again. She may sit immediately, or it might take another series of trials. When she sits down again, give another treat and see if you can scratch the dog gently without getting her riled up. After a few more successful trials, leave the lesson for the day.

Have different people do the approaching in your training sessions and conduct them in different locations so that the dog generalizes the idea. The more varied you can make the experience for the dog, the better. Once she is off-leash, if the dog attempts to jump up, turn your back.

 You Can Quote Me 99

Can dog owners solve a problem without understanding the reason behind it? Yes, easily, in most cases. I think the 'understanding' or analysis of the problem frequently gets in the way of actually solving it. People make excuses and allow problems to continue because they think they understand the reason for it.

Mandy Book

I prefer this method because you're letting the dog figure out the behavior that will be rewarded, rather than just making the dog obey a command. This way, once the behavior is ingrained, it will happen even in the absence of any command. This experiment is an example of cooperative communication. You are telling the dog, "I will give you want you want when you give me what I want."

Barking

As the saying goes, "Bees gotta buzz, dogs gotta bark." The problem comes in when we don't like when, where, how long and how often the barking occurs.

If you have a barking problem, I highly recommend Terry Ryan's book *The Bark Stops Here*. She explains the half-dozen major reasons

Trick training classes often include cute behaviors such as dancing.

that dogs bark excessively and ways to deal with each of them. This is beyond the scope of this book. What I *can* do here is talk about environmental enrichment (later in this chapter) because boredom and undirected energy are two major causes of barking. And I can also provide a strategy that can at least help to curtail barking when you're present with the dog. That strategy is to put barking on cue.

Putting barking on cue provides you with an on/off switch. Obviously, it won't work when you're not around, though it could possibly help your dog learn a little self-control.

If you have a barking problem, there are plenty of times when your dog barks. Whenever you see something you know is going to set your dog off—maybe the delivery person arriving or a loose-roaming neighborhood cat approaching—say "speak" (or whatever word you choose). If the dog has noticed something before you and already started barking, say your cue anyway. Let the dog bark a few times, wait for a momentary pause (the dog has to breathe in at some point), say "quiet," and offer the dog a food treat. The treat may need to be something especially tasty to get the dog's attention off of barking and onto eating. Something the dog has to chew will give you a longer period of quiet. Peanut butter can also be very useful, especially if you can safely smear some behind the dog's upper front teeth. The longer you can entice the dog to stop barking, the better your chances of success. If the dog stops barking and looks at you, waiting for her treat, when you say "quiet," you're gaining control. Congratulations.

Don't use a word for your "quiet" cue that you might be in the habit of shouting at the dog. (I don't advise shouting at the dog at all, but I know how frustrating barking can be.) Try something like "hush," which is pretty hard to yell.

SOME BASIC TRAINING/COMMUNICATION

A Few Training Definitions

I've already mentioned clicker training and shaping and several other training terms in this book. Before you tackle a few training sessions, here are descriptions of these techniques.

Lure and reward training is now used by most puppy class instructors and even in many more advanced classes. Lure training is precisely what its name implies—the handler uses a food treat (or toy), moving it so the dog will follow and perform the desired behavior. To have a dog sit, you hold the treat at the dog's nose, then move it back over the top of the dog's head. Because of the way dogs are built, when the dog lifts her nose to follow the treat, her bottom hits the ground. You then give the dog the treat as the reward. Later, you can add a verbal cue and voilà, you have a sit on command.

Clicker training refers to the use of a small noisemaking device as a marker or "bridge." You condition the dog to the clicker by clicking and then giving a treat for several short sessions. Then you can use the clicker to mark some behavior, or piece of behavior, that you want. The clicker is most useful in capturing fast-moving or precise behaviors because it is faster than a verbal cue. If you played the Training Game in Chapter 3, Conversation With a Canine, you have some experience with the clicker.

The clicker can be used in shaping a behavior (also what you were doing in the Training Game in Chapter 3). Shaping simply means that you first click an unrefined version or piece of the behavior you ultimately want. If you wanted your dog to turn her head as far left as she can, for example, you would start by clicking a slight head turn. Gradually, you raise the criteria, clicking only instances of the behavior that are closer to what you want. (For a complete primer on clicker training, read *Quick Clicks*, written with Mandy Book.)

For the training we will discuss here, you don't need a clicker—just some treats and toys.

Food Bowl Guarding

Dogs who decide to protect food bowls (or chew treats or even toys) are pretty common. Some behaviorists believe that because food is such an important item to dogs, they should not be disturbed when eating, but I can't agree. My thinking is more in line with the many trainers who regularly advise food bowl exercises for their clients.

It's true that dogs should ordinarily be uninterrupted while eating. But it's also true that a visiting child may run up to a dog eating dinner before anyone can intervene, or that a dog may pick up something when out for a walk that an owner needs to take away. Dogs need to understand that human intervention is not only to be accepted, but may even be enjoyable.

This is best done with puppies, but it can also be done with older dogs who show no resentment over interference with their food or possessions. If you already have a situation involving a dog growling over a food bowl or piece of rawhide, though, you need face-to-face help, an expert on-site to read the seriousness of the dog's intent and deal with it appropriately. The following exercises are for puppies or mild-mannered adults only.

Start the exercise nonconfrontationally by walking up to the dog while she is eating dinner and drop a yummy morsel into her bowl. Repeat this at every meal for several days. Then pick up the bowl to add the yummy morsel, and put it back down. Repeat this for several days.

Next, for several days, actually put your hand in the bowl, push the food around a little and leave an extra yummy morsel behind. Finally, hold the bowl and feed the dog piece by piece for awhile, right in the middle of the dog's dinner.

Remember throughout this procedure to watch what your dog is telling you. If, at any point, she gets stiff and tense, growls, stares at you and raises her hackles or otherwise communicates that she is not comfortable with what you're doing, back off and seek help. If you're dealing with a puppy, back up just one step—go back to dropping treats in the bowl while standing at your full height—and work each step for a longer period. Be sure you are training and socializing the puppy as well. For behavior around chews and toys, see the following sections on "give" and "off."

Give/Drop

The following exercises are for possessions other than the food bowl. The "give" or "drop" cue can make the game of fetch safer, rescue some possession that the dog has grabbed or maybe even save the dog's life if she's about to eat something toxic. It is an absolutely essential command if you wish to play tug with your dog.

A simple, stress-free way to teach "give" is to do toy exchanges. Play with a ball or a toy with your dog, but have a second toy nearby. After you've played for a little while, say "give" and whip out the

Even the British, famous for their well-mannered dogs who are allowed everywhere, recognize that some temptations are just too much for dogs to withstand.

second toy. Waggle it around and make it more enticing than the first toy (which you let go limp). Most dogs will grab for the second toy, thus releasing the first. Play with the second toy for a while, then you can do the exchange again, going back to the first toy. Your interaction with the toy is what increases its value, so you should be able to switch with no problem.

If your dog won't relinquish the toy, stop all interaction with her immediately. If this does not cause any consternation in your dog, then you have some sort of problem in your basic relationship and you need to attend to it before attempting other training. It may be that the dog views you as a subordinate rather than a benevolent leader, which can create serious problems.

Let's assume that all is going well and the dog is happily doing toy exchanges for you. After you've been working on this for several days, start saying "give" and waiting a few seconds before producing the second toy. If the dog releases on command, praise enthusiastically, give some treats, then play with the second toy. Asking a dog to give up possession of something she has in her mouth is asking a lot, so you should really make it worth the dog's while.

Keep practicing the give cue even after you've got it working well. You never know when you may need it.

Off/Leave It

This important cue has an almost Zenlike meaning—you must give something up to get it. This concept can be a tough one for human children to comprehend, let alone canine children.

Don't teach this concept until you have firmly established bite inhibition in your dog. You want to first impress the dog with how gentle she must be around humans before you don't let her touch you at all. Besides, you don't want to try this with a dog who might really try to get at what's in your hand.

Sit with your dog in a quiet place. Show her that you have a treat in your hand. If the dog reaches toward the treat, close your fingers over it *without* jerking your hand away and say "leave it." (Yanking your hand away will only convince your dog to try to be faster next time and will defeat the purpose of your training.) The dog may nuzzle or paw at your hand, but because you've taught bite inhibition, she shouldn't be obnoxious about it. Don't respond to anything she tries unless she gets so pushy that you need to yelp and remind her to be gentle. Sooner or later your dog will realize that what she's doing isn't working and will back off to rethink her strategy. When she does, say your release word, open your hand and let your dog have the treat. Sometimes, rather than giving the treat, grab a toy and play with the dog.

Most dogs are really confused by this exercise. The concept of *not* doing something—not pawing or mouthing at you—is more difficult than learning to do something, such as sitting.

You can transfer the command to items you aren't holding in your hand. Place a treat on the ground while the dog is watching. Say "leave it" and stand up straight. Be ready to put your foot over the treat if your dog goes for it. If you don't want the dog to ever pick up food off the ground, when the dog backs off, pick the treat up yourself before using your release word and letting the dog have it.

Dogs who have a lot of practice at these last two commands will actually drop fish bones they've found on the beach or stop short of picking up that unidentified thing lying on the path. You never know when you might need these commands, so keep them in good working order.

ENVRONMENTAL ENRICHMENT AND SEPARATION ANXIETY

In most families these days, everyone is either working, in school or in day care, and as a result, most dogs spend a great deal of their time home alone. Separation anxiety has become a major canine topic. Dogs are pack animals and never enjoy being left alone. Even if latchkey dogs don't show full-blown separation anxiety, they may take up the hobby of barking or digging. You wouldn't leave a two- or three-year-old child home alone all day with no one to supervise and nothing to do; so it's not surprising that a dog, whom researchers tell us has about the same mental capacity as a two- or three-year-old human, experiences problems in such circumstances.

To avoid separation anxiety in a puppy or to deal with it in an adult who's already showing signs, you need to gradually accustom the puppy or dog to being left alone. This is a time-consuming and often annoying process, but it will pay off with huge dividends if you hang in there and see it through.

Start by using a baby gate to block the dog into a separate room, but from which she can see you. Give her a stuffed Kong (see the following sidebar) or a special chew toy and go and sit down and read a book or watch television. Keep one eye on the pup just to see that she doesn't get into any trouble. Don't respond to any whining or carrying on. Wait until the dog is quiet before letting her rejoin you. Don't make a big fuss during the greeting. Repeat this sporadically, and the dog should eventually accept it without a fuss. When she can remain settled within sight of you, switch to a room from which the dog can't see you and do the whole routine all over again.

Try It Yourself

The Kong is a tough hollow rubber toy that looks sort of like a pinecone, and is perfect for occupying a dog. Fill it with some kibble, and peanut butter, cream cheese or cheese from a can. Present it to the dog before you leave, saying something like "I'll be back." If your dog is already suffering separation anxiety, it's likely she won't touch the Kong, but that's all right. You'll know you're making progress when the dog does eat something from the Kong while you're gone.

Slowly work up to leaving the dog in the out-of-sight room for half an hour. Once you've accomplished this, start actually leaving the house. Give the dog the stuffed Kong or chew toy but don't make a scene. Walk out and close the door behind you. Go only far enough to be out of the dog's sight because you're going to come back in 30 seconds. Don't make a big fuss when you come back in. Wait until the dog is calm before greeting her.

You're going to continue this procedure many times, slowly increasing the time you stay away every few days. Although most problems start soon after the owner leaves, 30 seconds is bearable for most dogs. If the dog hasn't destroyed anything or started barking while you were gone, extend your time away slightly. Try 45 seconds. When that is working, go for a full minute. You need to build up the separation time very gradually so you don't create more stress than your dog can handle. Take the dog with you if you need to go out for longer periods or you will risk setting back your training.

It takes weeks, but once you're up to a half hour, you may be able to run a quick errand while you're out. Dogs understand that you'll eventually return if you give them time to learn. It's the feeling of potential abandonment that seems to be the trigger behind separation anxiety, so if you can allay that feeling, you can avoid this problem.

The other way you can help dogs to be content on their own is to make their surroundings more rewarding. This can help not only with separation anxiety (though not if it's already established), but with barking, chewing, digging and maybe even escaping. You need to develop an enrichment plan that best suits you and your dog, but here are some ideas.

The game of treasure hunt lets your dog hunt for her dinner all through the house. Before you leave, put the dog outside or in the bathroom or have her practice a long down, while you hide kibble, biscuits and treats throughout the house and/or yard. Load up a Buster Cube or Kong and put that down as well. When you release the dog and leave, the dog can occupy herself with finding every last little morsel.

Dogs have to be taught to play this game, and you have to assess how vigorous your dog is about searching. You don't want to end up with broken possessions or a house that looks like it's been through an FBI evidence search! With those caveats, treasure hunt is a really fine way to give a dog something to do while you're absent, plus it teaches her to use her nose and mind.

Toys that can safely be left with the dog can be of immense benefit. Large, hard, nearly indestructible balls, originally designed to help keep horses from being bored, have become popular with dog owners. Try the toy out before leaving the dog home alone with it, though. My dog Spirit, the quintessential retriever, would cry and bark nonstop whenever she was presented with this object because she couldn't pick it up to retrieve it. Leaving her home alone with it would not have been popular with the neighbors. But many dogs quite happily play soccer with the thing, chasing it all over the yard and tiring themselves out nicely.

We devised our own toy for Starsky, a Puli mix who loved to jump. We hung a rope from the arbor over the back deck, to which we attached a spring and then one of those rubber ring tug toys. Starsky had to jump to reach the toy, but the spring then stretched enough for him to get his feet on the ground and tug. We watched him play with this contraption for a week before we decided it was safe enough for him to have on his own. The only problem we ever found was that sometimes the recoil when he let go was enough to shoot the whole contraption on top of the arbor. We'd really hear about this when we got home. (Pulis love to "talk" to their people, and he told us in no uncertain terms we needed to refine our design so his toy couldn't escape him.)

Think About It

Be creative and try out your own ideas. How does your dog most want to spend her time? Would a chair placed so she can see out the front window keep her quietly entertained or have her barking at everything that moves in the street? Know your dog and what will work for the both of you.

If your dog is not into ingesting such things as socks or strips of cloth, you can tie treats up in them (the more knots the better) and leave them for your dog to untie. You need to be certain that your dog will eat only the treat and leave the rest. Although socks might pass through the dog's digestive system and out the other end, they also might cause intestinal blockage and require surgery to remove.

If you are lucky enough to have a constant supply of cardboard boxes (and don't mind picking up the pieces at the end of the day), you can make a box riddle by putting small boxes inside larger ones with a nice hard chew inside the smallest box. For dogs who like to dissect, this is an excellent option.

Of course, having someone come in to exercise and entertain the dog during the day provides a nice break for the dog and burns off some energy. You can use professional, bonded and insured pet sitters/pet walkers, or you may know a responsible teenager in your neighborhood who might like to help you and your dog while earning a little cash.

Doggie day care has become popular in the last several years. You drop the dog off at a location in the morning and pick her up in the afternoon. In between, the staffers at the day care see to walks, play sessions with other dogs, rest periods and even meals if you like. Check out a dog day care just as you would for a child, since some are better than others. Visit any places you're considering to check for cleanliness and to see that play sessions are always supervised. Ask (and watch for) how many dogs one person walks at a time (no more than three is acceptable, and two is better). See if the staff has a system for logging dogs in and out so they know where each dog is at all times. Ask for references.

Finally, many people consider getting a second dog as a companion for the first one. Unfortunately, this idea usually crops up after the first dog has developed behavior problems of some sort, and the second dog is viewed as a "quick fix." What you will probably end up with in this case is two dogs with behavior problems.

However, a second dog can be an excellent addition if you go about things sensibly. I've found that dogs one to two years apart in age generally become very good friends. If there is a larger age difference, they may take longer to warm up to each other. If your dog is the original life of the party who tries to greet every dog she sees, a second dog may be a good choice for you. Proceed cautiously, however, and remember that your expenses will double. While you can probably walk both dogs at one time, they'll both crave and appreciate some one-on-one time. You'll also have to spend training time with each. If your second dog arrives as a puppy, be careful not to neglect your older dog in all the fuss over the new pup. This can lead to resentment.

Only my very first dog lived in a single-dog household, so I'm all in favor of dogs having other dogs around. But it's more work and more responsibility, as well as being more fun and more fulfilling.

Biscuits & Bath doggy day care in New York City, where the large dogs are having a play session. (The human supervisor is hiding behind one of the columns.)

SOME BASIC THINGS TO KEEP IN MIND

You are responsible for molding your dog into a model canine citizen. The dog doesn't come into your home knowing that some places are appropriate for pottying and others aren't, or some times are OK for barking but others aren't. You need to communicate the rules calmly and consistently.

Your dog is not a stuffed toy, meant to wait quietly in a corner until you feel like a little playtime. She requires regular checkups, a good diet, at least some basic training, daily interaction with her human pack and daily exercise. Any behaviors that create discord in the family or the neighborhood have to be resolved to everyone's satisfaction (including the dog's).

Some problems may require compromise. The dog can't help shedding, and if it upsets you to have dog hair "accessorizing" your outfit or to find dust bunnies behind every door, you either need to brush the dog more, dust and vacuum more or relax and realize that a little dog hair never killed anyone.

Some compromises are more serious. If the dog forgets all your training the second she spots a squirrel, your compromise can be this: When we're somewhere where it's safe for you to run after a squirrel and not come to me (such as out in the woods, where the squirrel can safely escape up a tree and there's no traffic to worry about), I won't try to call you or get upset when you don't listen. When we're somewhere where you can't go dashing off (a small city park surrounded by streets and used by families with children), I'll keep you on leash so that temptation won't overcome you. I won't lose my temper, but I will work on having you not lunge and bark, so that you learn a little self-control.

Other, more serious, problems don't allow for compromise and have to be managed. My dog Spirit, for example, was what I can best describe as psychotic. The victim of a puppy mill/pet shop upbringing, she had few social graces with dogs or humans, a fear of many things and a resolute determination to defend herself from all comers. I was responsible for managing her environment so that she was not put into situations with inevitably bad outcomes. She went to class every week for much of her life, and made as much progress as her scrambled brain circuits would permit. After 14 years of edgy

The inimitable Spirit, foreground (and the high-jumping Starsky).

living, Spirit went senile and suddenly became a kind and gentle dog who liked some people and tolerated most others. The final two and a half years of her time with us seemed like some sort of reward for all the trouble.

When faced with a problem, use what you've learned in these pages. Step back and focus on what's causing the problem, how the dog is being rewarded for the behavior and how you can counteract that reward and change the dog's viewpoint. Understanding and patience will usually get you where you want to go.

Remember your basic training alphabet:

A = Any rewards. Use rewards to manipulate your dog's behavior.

B = Better luck next time. This is what you're using when you turn and walk away in teaching the dog not to jump up.

C = Consequences or, more commonly, punishment. Notice that we've hardly mentioned it in all these pages.

D = Don't leave the dog under orders; remember to use your release word.

CHAPTER 12

Now We're Talking!

Are you more receptive to what your dog is trying to tell you?
Would you like some more ways to have fun with your dog?

> The fidelity of a dog is a precious gift demanding no less
> binding moral responsibilities than the friendship of a human
> being. The bond with a true dog is as lasting as the ties of this
> earth can ever be.
>
> Konrad Lorenz

The Seminoles have a variety of legends regarding dogs. But, as we're nearing the
end of the book, I'll tell you here the short tale of the paths through the sky. The
Seminoles believe that after death, if the rituals are done correctly, the human
spirit will travel the solopi heni, the Milky Way or Large White Spirit Way. They
also believe that the spirits of their deceased dogs travel the ifi heni, or Dog Way,
the little path through the sky. The solopi heni and ifi heni meet in the skies, so
that the humans and dogs may travel together to the good city of souls.

So, are you conversing with your dog more now? I hope so. Clear communication can avoid or resolve a lot of the most common problems between dogs and their humans, but it can also go far beyond that.

Even if you don't believe in telepathy, you can become more intuitive about your dog through close association. If you are used to observing your dog closely and regularly, you can catch many medical problems before they become serious and recognize when something is making her unhappy. Your dog probably does the same thing with you—this is why dogs so often appear to offer a paw or a lick when their human is feeling down.

You Can Quote Me

Dogs are better than us at a lot of things, and the lessons are all there for the taking if we'll take the time.
            Karen Overall, veterinarian, columnist and animal behaviorist

Your major responsibility is to keep the communication lines open between you and your dog. Communication with your canine is easier once you've laid down the basic framework, but you do have to continue working at it. One fun and easy way to do this is to keep learning new things together.

Think of couples you know. The most content nearly always are people who are out there trying new things, taking classes, joining clubs, traveling, exploring, reading, whatever. It's no different with people and their dogs. Doing things together and broadening horizons helps keep communication channels open and brain cells buzzing. Read the rest of this chapter for an introduction to the wide world of dog sports and other fun things for you and your dog to do together.

Many of the following ideas are organized dog sports with competition for ribbons and trophies. Remember to view them as fun things to do with your dog and avoid getting carried away with the competition aspect. Yes, winning is nice and trophies can be quite beautiful, but your dog is more beautiful and precious. If you keep remembering that, you'll always do fine, whether you come out of the ring at the top of your class or the bottom.

See the Resources section at the back of the book for further reading, sponsoring organizations and Web sites for any activities that strike your fancy.

AGILITY

Started as lunchtime entertainment at the Crufts dog show in Britain and still rising in popularity more than a dozen years later, agility tests the mental and physical abilities of dog and handler. Though many of the obstacles are the same for each outing, their order and presentation varies. To direct a dog through the tunnels, over the jumps, up the dog walk and A-frame, around the weave poles and across the seesaw in the correct order in a set amount of time requires clear communication, understanding of how the dog will see the course (course designers include "traps" for the unwary, where the most inviting next obstacle isn't the required one) and lots and lots of practice.

Most dogs really enjoy agility. While built-for-speed Border Collies, Shetland Sheepdogs and Jack Russell Terriers often dominate the winners' circles, I've seen Newfoundlands, Corgis and Basset Hounds compete with enthusiasm.

Because this is a highly active sport, check with your veterinarian first to be sure the jumping and climbing won't cause any problems for the dog before beginning training. The AKC and UKC both offer agility, and the USDAA and NADAC are dedicated solely to agility.

BACKPACKING/HIKING

Whether it's a stroll on the beach, a hike through the forest or a multiday backpacking expedition, dogs make terrific walking companions. They enjoy the great outdoors so much, and their enthusiasm is so contagious, that it seems to make the going easier.

On extended walks, dogs can easily fall victim to heatstroke in the warm weather that humans favor for hiking. Many dogs also want so much to please that they will struggle on even though they are suffering. You need to keep a sharp eye out for the dog's well-being.

If you are going backpacking, your dog can certainly help carry the load with a pack of her own. Get help making sure the pack fits well, and always be careful to balance the load between the two packs on either side.

CANINE GOOD CITIZEN (CGC)

This won't keep you occupied for very long because it's a test of basic good manners, and once you've passed, that's it. But it's a good way for everyone to take that first step into participating in a dog event, in a fairly nonthreatening atmosphere.

My Serling was part Newfoundland and enjoyed the beach above all else.

It's the only AKC-sponsored event that allows mixed breeds as well as purebreds. Local training clubs often offer a CGC test as graduation from a series of classes. The dog has to demonstrate abilities such as walking on a loose leash, accepting handling from a stranger, coming when called and remaining composed around people and things like bikes and shopping carts. Judges evaluate the dogs on a pass/fail basis, so there's no real competition, and a few townships or counties actually reward dog owners for achieving a CGC (either with a free license or increased off-leash freedom in parks). It may also come in handy if the company that insures your home ever gets the idea of objecting to dogs in the home.

CONFORMATION

This is the competition most regular folks think of when they hear "dog show," where dogs are judged on how they look. If you've watched television coverage of the Westminster Kennel Club show, you've seen conformation. It's a lot harder than it looks and takes

Even mixed breeds can compete in conformation through the Mixed Breed Dog Clubs of America. Judging is based on sound structure and good temperament. That's MB-Ch. Serling on the left and MB-Ch. Chewbaca on the right.

considerable practice together and a good understanding of what will keep your dog interested and enthusiastic.

The dogs are actually judged against the written standard for the breed, so you need a good specimen of your breed to have success. How well you work together with your dog in posing and moving and how much the dog enjoys the activity can also have a significant impact on the outcome.

Conformation is one of the more confusing sports to newcomers, so you will want to do some reading and studying and probably take some classes to be sure you know what you're doing. Many people make friends with other owners of their breed and see going to shows as a social outing as well as a chance to compete.

DRAFTWORK

Away from the snowy realms of sled dog racing (which we'll talk about later), there are two basic sorts of draftwork. Carting competitions are not a frequent event in many areas, but the breed clubs for dogs that traditionally did this sort of work—Bernese Mountain Dogs and Newfoundlands, for example—do hold trials to test the dogs' abilities. Most carting trials consist of a test of maneuvering skill in tight quarters and a test of stamina and actual working ability along an extended course through varied terrain and distractions.

Weight pulling is an entirely different event, a challenge to determine how much weight a dog can pull over a short straight distance on a cart or sled. The International Weight Pulling Association runs these events. The dogs are never allowed to fail, receiving human help in moving the load, if necessary, before being unhitched. You should, of course, be certain that your dog is physically fit before attempting such a strenuous activity.

EARTHDOG

Also known as go-to-grounds or terrier trials, this sport is meant for those dogs who were bred to go down holes after "vermin." Not all terriers qualify because some are too large to fit into the nine-by-nine-inch hole. And earthdog is not only for terriers—Dachshunds are included as well.

The trials test a dog's natural instincts, so you can start competing without any training. A trench is dug and covered with a wooden structure and branches. A caged rat is placed at the end and a scent trail is laid. When the dog is released, she's expected to follow the scent trail down the tunnel to the end and then "worry" the rat by barking and digging. Terrier trials often also include racing the dogs (see the Racing section).

FIELD

Pointers, retrievers, spaniels, setters, coonhounds, Beagles and even Airedale Terriers (with the UKC) have their own special field events. Most have instinct tests that don't require a lot of training. Beagles, Basset Hounds and Dachshunds compete in trailing trials, instinctively using their noses to track the quarry (usually rabbits) in the field. Night hunts, pointing trials and retriever trials require stamina, precision, good communication and many hours of training to have any hope of winning.

Pointing trials include Brittanys, Pointers, German Pointers (both shorthaired and wirehaired), Vizslas, Weimaraners, Wirehaired Pointing Griffons and the setters (English, Gordon and Irish). Here you will often find "field-bred" dogs that look somewhat different from their brethren appearing in the show ring. Field dogs often have less full coats, are smaller or lighter and have broader heads. These wide-ranging dogs require that handlers and judges follow on horseback to keep up.

Retriever trials include all the retrievers plus Irish Water Spaniels. There are far more Labradors in competition than any other breed. These dogs are expected to retrieve birds both on land and in water. Owners have their choice of working certificate programs, AKC hunting tests or field trials (for the highly trained and very serious).

All the spaniels are eligible to compete in spaniel trials, but only English Springer Spaniels compete with any regularity. Spaniels are expected to find birds, flush them for the handler to shoot and then retrieve them to the handler. The coonhounds compete in Night Hunts, trailing and treeing raccoons. These events are one of the most popular dog contests offered by the UKC.

FLYBALL

Flyball is a relay race for dogs, many of whom seem to become quite addicted to the chaos and excitement. Two teams race directly against each other down a straight course over four low hurdles to a box, where they must trigger and catch a tennis ball and return over the jumps. As one dog finishes, the next dog sets out, until all four team members have completed their runs.

The dogs have to be trained to play this game by the rules. But if you've ever watched (and heard) the enthusiasm before and during a run, you may be inspired to try it.

FREESTYLE

One of the newest sports is freestyle, or dancing with your dog. Combining obedience and trick training moves, a handler choreographs routines to music, with a dog as his partner. Based loosely on the

A moment from an early freestyle performance. Note the costuming, the spectators and the dog's grin.

world of figure skating, there are noncompetitive proficiency tests and several competitive divisions.

Freestyle involves plenty of training, but the sport seems to attract camaraderie—small groups of enthusiasts often get together to try things out, practice new moves or present routines in public for the first time. Any size or shape of breed or mixed breed is welcome. Since the sport is so new, events are still relatively rare, but the World Canine Freestyle Organization (WCFO) acknowledges this by accepting videotaped entries for special video competitions.

FUN RUNS

A variety of charitable organizations use fun runs/walks as a way to raise money, and some of these events welcome dogs. Some benefit humane societies or other dog-related causes, and these may include extra added attractions such as talent or other competitions.

Not much training is required for this. Because these walks can often be crowded, your dog should be well socialized and should be able to walk well on leash. If the walk is a long one, be sure you're both in good enough shape to handle it, and be careful of hot weather.

HERDING

You might think this activity is only for the dogs in the Herding Group, but (at least as far as the American Herding Breeds Association goes), you'd be wrong. Some breeds from the Working Group, some from Non-Sporting and even mixed breeds are eligible. AHBA's focus is on the work, and they're not that particular about the dogs who do it. The U.S. Border Collie Handlers Association also allows any dog capable of doing the work into their trials (though they also claim that, mostly, only Border Collies are capable).

You can take an instinct test with only some basic obedience training, under the watchful eye of an experienced handler, so there's no danger to the livestock. Anything beyond this requires plenty of training and an understanding not only of your dog but also of the livestock you will be working (which is usually sheep, but could also be cows, goats or ducks).

LURE COURSING

The sighthounds from the Hound Group are the specialists of this sport, and Whippets are probably the most frequent competitors. These dogs were bred to chase and run down game in the field, whether jackrabbits, gazelle or deer. The National Open Field Coursing Association (NOFCA) still operates this way, but only in the few states where it's legal.

The American Sighthound Field Association (ASFA) uses lures rather than live game, making it legal everywhere (and more palatable to many people). Local clubs will sometimes have fun runs, where people with hounds can try out the sport.

The dogs are examined before the runs begin to check that all are in good physical condition. Lots are drawn to see who will run together, and two or three dogs of the same breed usually run at once. The dogs are not allowed to interfere with one another on the course, and much of the training lies in convincing the excited dogs to allow themselves to be captured at the end of the run!

Papillons make great little obedience competitors, as do many other breeds not commonly thought of as "obedience dogs."

OBEDIENCE

Probably the third oldest of the official dog sports, behind field trials and conformation, obedience tests the training and teamwork of handler and dog. Some breeds are generally more "biddable" (easy to train) than others, and you'll often see Border Collies and Golden Retrievers pulling down the big trophies at obedience trials. But any breed can compete successfully in obedience. The handler simply has to understand how to motivate the dog. A Beagle isn't going to ignore all those enticing smells on the ground to do some silly heeling pattern unless you provide a reason that makes sense to the dog. In fact, unless you're smart enough to motivate them, a lot of hounds just don't see the point in obeying commands at all. Fortunately, many of them really appreciate food treats.

There are various levels of competition in obedience, as there are in most sports. The Novice level tests the dog's heeling abilities, plus a recall (staying and coming when called), standing still and allowing the judge to touch her and staying in a "sit" for one minute and a "down" for three minutes. More advanced levels add jumping, retrieving, silent exercises and other such challenges.

PET THERAPY

Not exactly a sport, but it's certainly a way to better appreciate the bond between people and dogs. Pet therapy as it's generally used means taking your dog to visit people in such places as convalescent centers, hospices, hospitals and so on. Your dog must be well behaved because even an accidental scratch with a toenail could be serious for some patients. She must also be clean and free of fleas.

The Delta Society has quite an intensive training program (covering both the dog and the human sides of the partnership) that will inform you what to expect and how to conduct yourself. Once you are certified, you are covered under the Delta Society insurance policy.

You and your dog might choose to simply provide a furry body to snuggle and give affection, or you can put on little shows and demonstrations in the activity rooms of the places you visit.

RACING

Unlike sled dog racing, this event is held on snow-free ground. A variety of breed clubs sponsor races for their dogs. Dachshunds race on the flat, whereas Jack Russell Terriers race both on the flat and over hurdles. Whippets and Greyhounds race on straightaways or around ovals. (This competition bears no relation to commercial Greyhound racing—these are fun events meant to give the dogs another chance to show their speed, with nothing more than ribbons up for the taking.) Some training is involved, mainly to keep dogs from interfering with one another, but generally the dogs' desire to run takes over.

SCHUTZHUND

This is a serious multifaceted sport that requires a great deal of dedication and training. Schutzhund competition consists of three parts: obedience, tracking and protection work. The obedience and tracking are both somewhat different from the AKC variety.

The AKC frowns on this sport, citing vague concerns about aggression in the protection phase. If you investigate a little further, you'll find that the dogs aren't being aggressive at all—their trainers are tapping into the dogs' natural instincts in a supremely controlled way, as in earthdog, lure coursing, field trials and just about every other canine sport. In fact, many of the dogs *love* the "bad guy" wearing the protective sleeve and wouldn't dream of biting anything other than that sleeve. The dogs have to let go immediately on command, as well as guard a human subject without biting the sleeve. Schutzhund will certainly test your ability to communicate with your dog, but not all dogs are right for this sport. Good temperament is a must, and the training is rigorous.

SLED DOG RACING AND SKIJORING

Sled dog racing is what most people might think of when you mention dog racing. The Iditarod is the most famous race, since it's televised and followed by the media each year, but there are plenty of other races almost anywhere there is snow and open space.

The International Sled Dog Racing Association doesn't care about the lineage of the dogs in harness—mixed breeds are popular, and there have been teams of Poodles and Dalmatians.

There are races of various lengths, with different numbers of dogs doing the pulling. You have to condition and train dogs to perform this activity, and you have to understand each dog's personality to know where in the team she will best fit.

Skijoring is a more personal, noncompetitive sport, where a single dog or a couple are in harness pulling a human on cross-country skis.

TRACKING

Tracking uses the dog's excellent sense of smell to follow a scent trail left by a human. Both the AKC and UKC offer several levels of tracking tests, all of which are pass/fail.

Though dogs certainly know how to follow a scent, they have to be trained to track for competition because they must follow the ground scent rather than the airborne scent. (The details of scent and how it moves through the environment are a book in itself.) Judges want the dog's nose on the ground, not up in the air. The dog must also indicate (by sitting or lying down or standing and barking) several articles left along the track.

TRICK TRAINING/TALENT COMPETITIONS

Teaching your dog some tricks is a great way to keep the communication lines open and make training fun for everyone. You can use tricks in pet therapy, in freestyle and in a variety of other venues.

Serling, who had a role in a movie despite being black and hard to photograph, demonstrating "Wave."

They're terrific as part of a school visit program (where dog owners educate elementary school children on how to behave around dogs).

Talent competitions for dogs may be part of county or state fairs, charity dog walks or canine "Olympics" or other just-for-fun events. You might win a blue ribbon, some dog-related goodies such as bowls and leashes, a supply of dog food or even cash.

WATER WORK

Water rescue work was originally the purview of Newfoundlands and Portuguese Water Dogs, since these breeds were developed to assist humans with tasks in the water. Portuguese Water Dogs helped fishermen to tow nets and even retrieve fish or items that had fallen in the water. Newfoundlands were historically more focused on rescue work.

A Belgian Tervuren and a mixed breed practice their water retrieves.

The breed clubs for these two breeds hold events for their dogs, while a group called Wet Dog received permission from the Newfoundland Club of America to adapt their test for all dogs to attempt.

If you join in this activity, plan on getting wet. You'll need to encourage the dog to tow a boat and retrieve a floating object. You'll also have to swim with the dog and be "rescued." Training is a lot of fun for all involved if you live in a warm-weather area.

OTHER ACTIVITIES

This list isn't comprehensive, it's just a starting point to get you and your dog going on canine activities. There's also Frisbee competition, Roading for Dalmatians and search-and-rescue (a serious, intense, time-consuming, but valuable way for you and your dog to make a contribution), to name but a few. Many breeds have specific "versatility" programs. Look around and choose something that appeals to you and your dog. It will help keep the communication lines open, and you and your dog will enjoy each other.

Resources

BOOKS

The Absolute Beginner's Guide to Showing Your Dog, Cheryl S. Smith, Prima Publishing, 2001.

The Angell Memorial Animal Hospital Book of Wellness and Preventive Care for Dogs, Darlene Arden, Contemporary Books, 2003.

The Animal Attraction, Jonica Newby, ABC Books, 1997.

Applied Dog Behavior and Training, Steven R. Lindsay, Iowa State University Press, 2000.

The Bark Stops Here, Terry Ryan, Legacy-By-Mail, 2000.

The Body Language and Emotion of Dogs, Myrna Milani, William Morrow & Co., 1986.

Body Posture and Emotions, Suzanne Clothier, Flying Dog Press, 1996.

Bones Would Rain from the Sky, Suzanne Clothier, Warner Books, 2002.

Canine Behavior: A Guide for Veterinarians, Bonnie Beaver, W.B. Saunders, 1999.

Canine Massage: A Practical Guide, Jean-Pierre Hourdebaigt and Shari L. Seymour, Howell Book House, 1999.

Clicker Training for Obedience, Morgan Spector, Sunshine Books, 1999.

Complete Care for Your Aging Dog, Amy Shojai, New American Library, 2003.

Culture Clash, Jean Donaldson, James & Kenneth Publishers, 1996.

Dog Behavior, Ian Dunbar, Howell Book House, 1999.

Dog Friendly Gardens, Garden Friendly Dogs, Cheryl S. Smith, Dogwise, 2003.

A Dog Is Listening, Roger Caras, Fireside, 1992.

Dog Language, Roger Abrantes, Wakan Tanka Publishers, 1997.

Dog Training: The Gentle Modern Method, David Weston, Howell Book House, 1990.

The Domestic Dog, James Serpell, Cambridge University Press, 1995.

The Evolution of Canine Social Behavior, Wakan Tanka Publishers, 1997.

Finding a Balance, Suzanne Clothier, Flying Dog Press, 1996.

How to Teach a New Dog Old Tricks, Ian Dunbar, James & Kenneth, 1991.

The Inducive Retrieve, Sue Sternberg, self-published, 1995.

On Talking Terms with Dogs: Calming Signals, Turid Rugaas, Legacy-By-Mail, 1997.

The Other End of the Leash, Patricia McConnell, Ballantine Books, 2002.

Quick Clicks, Mandy Book and Cheryl S. Smith, HanaleiPets, 2001.

The Trick Is in the Training, Cheryl S. Smith, Barron's, 1998.

The Waltham Book of Dog and Cat Behaviour, Pergamon Press, 1992.

The Waltham Book of Human-Animal Interaction, Pergamon Press, 1995.

VIDEOS

Bodywork for Dogs, Lynn Vaughan and Deborah Jones (animalhealing.com)

Calming Signals: What Your Dog Tells You, Turid Rugaas

CANINE REGISTRIES AND KENNEL CLUBS

American Kennel Club
260 Madison Avenue
New York, NY 10016
www.akc.org

United Kennel Club
100 Kilgore Road
Kalamazoo, MI 49002
www.ukcdogs.com

Federation Cynologique Internationale
Place Albert I
13 B-6530 Thuin, Belgium
www.fci.be

American Mixed Breed Obedience Registry
179 Niblick Road, #113
Paso Robles, CA 93446
www.amborusa.org

DOG TRAINERS' ASSOCIATIONS

Association of Pet Dog Trainers
P. O. Box 1781
Hobbs, NM 88241
www.apdt.com

North American Dog Obedience Instructors
PMB #369
729 Grapevine Highway, Suite 369
Hurst, TX 76054
www.nadoi.org

WEB SITES

www.writedog.com
Cheryl Smith's Web site, from which you can e-mail her

Clicker Training

clickandtreat.com
Gary Wilkes' clicker training site

www.bestbehavior.net
Morgan Spector's clicker training site

www.clickersolutions.com
Bob and Marian Bailey and others on clicker training

Massage

www.amtamassage.org
American Massage Therapy Association

www.integratedanimal.com
Lauren McCall and Debby Potts on animal communication and massage

Dog Books and Other Stuff

www.dogwise.com
A canine bookseller and more, with most of the products mentioned in this
book

www.hanaleipets.com
A supplier of dog treats, training items, books and videos

Dog Events

www.puppyworks.com
A canine events planner, with information on upcoming lectures, conferences, etc.

www.legacycanine.com
Legacy's Web site, with information on seminars and lectures

Dog Sports

www.usdaa.com
www.nadac.com
Agility

www.cartingwithyourdog.com, iwpa.net
Draft work

www.dog-play.com/cgc.html
Information on the Canine Good Citizen program, and many links to
dog activity sites

www.dirt-dog.com/awta/index.shtml
Earthdog

www.nahra.org, americanfield.com
Field tests and trials for hunting dogs

www.flyball.org
Flyball

www.woofs.org/wcfo/
Freestyle

www.discdog.com/FAQ.htm
Frisbee

www.stockdog.com, primenet.com/~joell/ahba/main.htm
Herding

www.asfa.org
Lure coursing

www.deltasociety.org
Pet therapy

www.notra.org, terrier.com/trial/racing.php3
Racing

www.k9web.com/dog-faqs/activities/schutzhund.html, germanshepherddog.com
Schutzhund

www.isdra.org, ooowoo.com
Sled dog racing and skijoring

www.wetdog.org, dogscouts.com/wet.shtml
Water work

Some Quotable People

I interviewed or consulted with most of the following people in writing this book. They were gracious enough to provide a wealth of information. Some are quoted from their published works.

Roger Abrantes

Roger Abrantes is an ethologist and scientific director of the Institute of Ethology at the Hong Agriculture School in Denmark. He is author of more than a dozen books and a well-known international lecturer.

Bob and Marian Bailey, Ph.D.

Marian Bailey founded Animal Behavior Enterprises (ABE) with her first husband, Keller Breland. They trained many species of animals for both commercial and secret government work, using the principles of operant conditioning. Bob Bailey, a chemist and zoologist, became General Manager of ABE, and after Keller died, became Marian's second husband. Together, they trained thousands of animals, served as media consultants and finally began training other trainers at world-renowned camps. Marian passed away in 2001, but Bob continues sharing his knowledge with dog trainers and others.

Bonnie Beaver

Bonnie Beaver, MS, DVM, is chief of medicine in the Department of Small Animal Medicine and Surgery at the College of Veterinary Medicine, Texas A&M University. She writes and lectures on canine behavior.

Mandy Book

Mandy Book has been training dogs for 15 years. She recently sold her ten-year-old dog training business and now works for Sirius Puppy Training in the San Francisco Bay area. Her training focus is on humane methods that treat the dog as a partner, rather than as an adversary. She has a varied background in dogs, which includes working with dogs in print ads and books, training a variety of breeds from humane society rescues to assistance dogs and training chickens. She is also a contributing editor for *The Healing Paw* (a newsletter for facility dogs). She lives with three dogs and her husband in San Jose.

Suzanne Clothier

Suzanne Clothier is author of many interesting books on our relationships with dogs, and a frequent lecturer at the annual Association of Pet Dog Trainers conference. Her holistic outlook on the bond between humans and other animals resonates through her writing and her dog training.

Raymond Coppinger

Ray Coppinger is professor of biology at Hampshire College. He was founder of the Livestock Dog Project and is a former sled dog racing champion. His most recent book explores his theory of how dogs became domesticated.

Jean Donaldson

Jean Donaldson is a dog class instructor, lecturer at the Association of Pet Dog Trainers and author of eye-opening books about dogs. She now works at the San Francisco SPCA, where she leads and instructs classes ranging from long weekends to six-week "boot camps" on dogs.

Ian Dunbar, Ph.D., MRCVS

Ian Dunbar is a veterinarian and animal behaviorist, host of a popular English television series and author of many fine dog books. An early proponent of positive training, Ian was instrumental in founding the Association of Pet Dog Trainers. He is the director of Sirius Puppy Training, and an internationally known lecturer on matters related to dogs.

Kerrie Haynes-Lovell

Kerrie Haynes-Lovell is assistant curator of Sea World Australia, involved in understanding and communicating with a variety of animal species. She recently was responsible for the installation of a new polar bear exhibit. She also lectures on understanding and working with dogs.

Margaret Johnson

Margaret Johnson has studied with some of the best trainers and behaviorists in the world, including Terry Ryan, Ian Dunbar, Erich Klinghammer, Patricia

McConnell and Morgan Spector. The gentle, positive methods she has learned are especially helpful in her extensive work with shy and fearful dogs. In 1998, Margaret helped to develop the obedience program at the Humane Society of Austin & Travis County and taught there for two years. She moved to a small ranch in Austin with her husband Rob, dogs Trudy and Gus and cat Edsel, and opened her own training business, "The Humaner Trainer," offering group and private lessons, workshops and behavior consultations. Johnson currently serves as Chair of the Sponsorship Committee for the Association of Pet Dog Trainers.

Lauren McCall

Lauren McCall is an animal communicator who also lectures on the subject to groups. She believes that in order to communicate you have to make a heart connection with the animal, and she helps people to find that better communication. She is also a Ttouch practitioner.

Patricia McConnell, Ph.D.

Patricia McConnell is a certified Applied Animal Behaviorist and an adjunct assistant professor of zoology at the University of Wisconsin-Madison. She hosts a syndicated radio show giving behavior advice, and lectures at a variety of venues.

Karen Overall, VMD

Karen Overall received her B.A. and M.A. degrees concomitantly, followed by her VMD, all from the University of Pennsylvania. She also has a Ph.D. in Zoology from the University of Wisconsin-Madison, and completed a residency in Behavioral Medicine at the University of Pennsylvania in 1989. She is an international lecturer and author, and a Diplomat of the American College of Veterinary Behavior. Overall is also certified by the Animal Behavior Society as an Applied Animal Behaviorist. She ran the Behavior Clinic at the University of Pennsylvania School of Veterinary Medicine for many years.

Debby Potts

Debby Potts has 17 years experience with the TTouch method. She teaches workshops and works privately with individuals in the United States, Europe, Japan and South Africa. She was also one of Oregon's first board-certified licensed veterinary technicians. Debby has always been concerned with animal health and behavior, and TTouch has allowed her to extend that care to improving the lives of animals and their people on a physical, spiritual and emotional level.

Karen Pryor

Karen Pryor did graduate work in zoology before shifting focus to become a dolphin trainer at Hawaii's Sea Life Park. She was one of the first to lecture widely on using clicker training with dogs, and has written books about her experiences with dolphins and clicker training in general.

Pamela Reid, Ph.D.

Pamela Reid is a psychologist specializing in animal learning and behavior. She is a certified applied animal behaviorist with a private practice dedicated to helping dog owners work out problems with their pets.

Turid Rugaas

Turid Rugaas is a Norwegian dog training instructor who has observed canine behavior for years and has identified what she believes are calming signals among dogs. She wrote a book on the subject and lectures internationally.

Terry Ryan

Terry Ryan is the president of Legacy Canine Behavior and Training, Inc. A busy international workshop presenter, Terry also hosts frequent camps and seminars taught by well-known dog experts from around the world. She spends several months a year in Japan teaching various dog training and instructor programs. Terry was coordinator of the People-Pet Partnership, College of Veterinary Medicine, Washington State University. She is a charter member of the Association of Pet Dog Trainers, past president and board member of the National Association of Dog Obedience Instructors and a regular contributor to the training column of the *AKC Gazette.*

Kathy Sdao

Kathy Sdao earned a master's in experimental psychology and put it to use with dolphins, first at the University of Hawaii's Kewalo Basin Marine Mammal Laboratory, then for the U.S. Navy and finally with a greater variety of marine mammals at Washington's Point Defiance Zoo and Aquarium. She opened the first doggy day care in Tacoma with a partner, and began teaching people how to "dolphin-train" their dogs. Now she specializes in private lessons, behavior modification and public speaking.

Morgan Spector

Morgan Spector has been a clicker trainer since 1993 and is the author of *Clicker Training for Obedience*. Morgan's training and teaching covers obedience competition, pet ownership, agility and service dog work. Morgan has also recently become involved in a program with the Pryor Foundation applying clicker training to work with families that have been victimized by domestic violence and child abuse. He operates Best Behavior Dog Training in Agua Dulce, California, where he lives with his wife and son, three dogs and a fluctuating population of outdoor cats.

Linda Tellington-Jones

Linda Tellington-Jones is a dedicated horsewoman, competing in all sorts of equestrian events worldwide. She developed a method of working with horses known as TEAM, Tellington-Jones Equine Awareness Method. She later adapted the touch work to other animals, and it became known as TTouch.

Dennis Wilcox, DVM

Dennis Wilcox received his B.A. from Western Washington University and his B.S. and DVM from Washington State University. He is also certified in medical *qi gong* from Master Wan at the Military Hospital for Paralysis in Beijing, China, and in veterinary herbal medicine by the Healing Oasis and Wellness Center in Sturdevant, Wisconsin. He has completed NET chiropractic techniques with Dr. Scott Walker, and is currently working on a certification in acupuncture. He has been in practice in Port Angeles, Washington, for 21 years, running an integrated conventional/alternative medicine small animal practice.

Gary Wilkes

Gary Wilkes is an internationally respected animal behaviorist, trainer and pioneer of clicker training—the first practical translation of operant conditioning for pet dogs and their owners. He has been a columnist in dog magazines and newspapers, and a popular lecturer.

Index